QuiStain®able Business Solutions

VISTEM

PROJECTS that FLOW
Win-Win Solutions

A workbook for solving dilemmas and conflict situations effectively

Thinking processes—Theory of Constraints (TOC)

ibidem

Band 6

QuiStain®able Business Solutions

Herausgeber: VISTEM

ISSN 2199-2975

VISTEM

PROJECTS that FLOW

WIN-WIN SOLUTIONS

A workbook for solving dilemmas and conflict situations effectively

Thinking processes—Theory of Constraints (TOC)

ibidem-Verlag

Stuttgart

Bibliografische Information der Deutschen Nationalbibliothek

Die Deutsche Nationalbibliothek verzeichnet diese Publikation in der Deutschen Nationalbibliografie; detaillierte bibliografische Daten sind im Internet über http://dnb.d-nb.de abrufbar.

Bibliographic information published by the Deutsche Nationalbibliothek

Die Deutsche Nationalbibliothek lists this publication in the Deutsche Nationalbibliografie; detailed bibliographic data are available in the Internet at http://dnb.d-nb.de.

∞

Gedruckt auf alterungsbeständigem, säurefreien Papier
Printed on acid-free paper

ISSN: 2199-2975
ISBN-13: 978-3-8382-0961-6

© *ibidem*-Verlag

Stuttgart 2016
Alle Rechte vorbehalten

Das Werk einschließlich aller seiner Teile ist urheberrechtlich geschützt. Jede Verwertung außerhalb der engen Grenzen des Urheberrechtsgesetzes ist ohne Zustimmung des Verlages unzulässig und strafbar. Dies gilt insbesondere für Vervielfältigungen, Übersetzungen, Mikroverfilmungen und elektronische Speicherformen sowie die Einspeicherung und Verarbeitung in elektronischen Systemen.

All rights reserved. No part of this publication may be reproduced, stored in or introduced into a retrieval system, or transmitted, in any form, or by any means (electronical, mechanical, photocopying, recording or otherwise) without the prior written permission of the publisher. Any person who does any unauthorized act in relation to this publication may be liable to criminal prosecution and civil claims for damages.

Printed in the EU

Contents

1 Dilemmas, decision-making and response conflicts 7

Dilemma

2 List of problems 9
3 Dilemma—exercise 1 (with full instructions) 11
4 Dilemma—exercise 2 (with full instructions) 29
5 Dilemma—exercise 3 47
6 Dilemma—exercise 4 57
7 Dilemma—exercise 5 67
8 Dilemma—summary and instructions for completion 77

Fire

9 Fire (inconsistency between tasks and competences) 79
10 Fire—exercise 1 (with full instructions) 81
11 Fire—exercise 2 89
12 Fire—summary and completion 95

Conflicts

13 Conflict 97
14 List of conflicts 99
15 Conflict—exercise 1 (with full instructions) 101
16 Conflict—exercise 2 113
17 Presenting Clouds.. 121

1 Dilemmas, decision-making and response conflicts

Decision-making conflicts (dilemmas) and conflicts between people and departments are everyday occurrences.

Again and again situations occur where someone has to decide between two or more alternative courses of action. The courses of action are mutually exclusive—only one can be realized. There are good reasons for and equally good reasons against each of the alternative courses of action. In other words, whatever you decide to do—it would seem to be—a mistake. Conflicts between two people, groups, or departments are just as common. One party advocates a specific action; they have good reasons for stating that this (and only this) course of action is suitable for achieving the (corporate) target. The other party advocates an alternative approach; they also have good reasons for their choice of action and equally good reasons why the other course of action is wrong and harmful.

The existence of such dilemmas and conflicts has consequences. The respective 'system' (e.g. an individual or a company) cannot achieve its objectives, without limitations.

The Theory of Constraints, within which the presented techniques have been developed, is based among other things, on the assumption that there is a win-win-solution for each conflict, a solution that allows the system to achieve more of its goals without creating a loser within the system.

With this workbook, you can train in the necessary skills to make conflicts and decision-making dilemmas transparent and find win-win solutions. It does not claim to be a complete and comprehensive compendium for conflict resolution.

1.1 The Conflict Resolution Diagram or Evaporating Cloud

The Evaporating Cloud, sometimes also referred to as a Conflict Resolution Diagram, is used for structured analysis and solutions to a problem situation. As part of the analysis, you describe the conflict, represent it graphically and examine it. As part of the solution, you search and test basic ways (solution directions) in which the dilemma/conflict can be resolved. The cloud then effectively evaporates into thin air.

The method is based on the following assumptions:
- All problems are based on conflict (conflict between alternative courses of action).
- There are no 'natural, irresolvable conflicts'.
- The cause for conflict lies in at least one false assumption.
- A solution without compromise, in which everybody benefits ('win-win'), is always possible.

Typical applications for the Evaporating Cloud include:
- Uncovering assumptions that underlie a conflict
- Resolving conflicts without compromise by separating motives
- Developing breakthrough-type solutions
- Managing negotiations with win-win for mutual satisfaction
- Solving internal conflicts ('what should I do?') and conflicts between individuals or groups

1.2 Types

In this book, you can learn and practice techniques for the resolution of conflicts based on three dilemmas—or types of conflict, each handled with a specific type of basic Conflict Cloud.

1.2.1 Evaporating Cloud

A person carries the dilemma within themselves, they could carry out both courses of action, however they are mutually exclusive. The person must choose one of the options.

1.2.2 Fire Cloud

A person wants to achieve a goal within a system (e.g. as an employee in a company) and to achieve this has to act in a certain way. However, the person is trapped in a dilemma, because a rule of the system prohibits this effective action. The person is unable to carry out effective action due to their position or role, and must turn to a higher level, to obtain a decision and backing.

1.2.3 Conflict Cloud

In a classic conflict situation, two people (or groups) face each other, both sides want to take actions that are exclusive. Actions will include preconditions necessary for achieving a common goal. The common goal may not be known at the beginning of the confrontation. Under certain circumstances, there may also turn out (initially) to be no common goal.

2 List of problems

In order that you can learn the techniques presented in this workbook, you first need training materials in the form of a list of properly formulated problems.

2.1 Instructions

1. Draw up a list of five recent situations that were stressful, because you had a decision dilemma:
   - On the one hand, there was pressure to do something.
   - On the other hand you would have preferred to do something else.

2. For this first exercise, select problems that are current, rather than those that are constantly recurring.

   Example of a current problem:
   - My boss wanted me to immediately take care of a request by customer Y.

   An example of a recurring problem:
   - We always have the problem, that we are unable to reply promptly to customer queries.

3. Summarize each problem in one sentence.

2.2 Examples of recently occurring problems

- My father wants me to clean up my room, but I would rather play.
- Andrea and I want to rent a holiday home in X and we are unable to choose between two offers.
- I was given a task that would be impossible for me to complete in the allotted time.
- My boss has not campaigned aggressively enough to secure an additional employee for my project team.
- Thomas is interfering in my work and brings my role as project manager into question.
- I had no access to the specifications that were absolutely necessary for the project.

Workbook Win-Win Solutions

2.3 My list of problems (recent problems)

1.	
2.	
3.	
4.	
5.	
6.	
7.	
8.	
9.	

Now, for your first exercise, select a problem from this list, which is not chronic, is in the past, and is completed. You will work on this problem in the following steps.

3 Dilemma — exercise 1 (with full instructions)

3.1 Problem report

The Problem Report helps you put your thoughts on the selected problem, as well as the facts, on paper, so they can be subsequently processed and structured.

3.1.1 Instructions

Write a report on your problem — as if you were writing an essay or a letter of complaint. In the report, explain why this situation presents a problem, and how you and your services will be/were affected.

Take into account the following questions:
- Who are the participants?
- What happened?
- When, and in what context did the situation occur?
- Where did it happen?
- What did I want to do? Why?
- What should I not do? Why?

3.1.2 Example of a problem report

Title / topic	Andrea and I want to rent a holiday home in X and we can't choose between offers.
Report	Andrea and I have been looking for a holiday home for a long time, now we have two interesting offers. On the one hand, a one bedroom apartment in X, and on the other, a larger two bedroom apartment in the neighboring village with a lake view. The apartment in X is located in the town center with restaurants and shops, a few minutes walk from the train station, and it would be possible to arrive by train every hour until one o'clock in the morning. I also find the price quite reasonable. We can only reach the neighboring village by means of an inconvenient bus connection or taxi. Andrea is worried, however, that it might be a tight squeeze in a one-bedroom apartment. Therefore, she prefers the location on the outskirts by the lake in the neighboring village, where she believes she will be able to relax better. Of course, we could decide on neither and wait for an even better deal. Recently we have fought a few times on this issue and I'm worried that our relationship could really suffer. Now, I don't know what action to take.

3.1.3 My problem report

Title / topic	
Report	

3.2 Possible actions

3.2.1 Instructions

1. Create a list of possible actions.

   Consider:
   - Actions which you think or would have thought are right.
   - Actions which others or 'the system' expect of you.

2. Write a short, clear sentence for each possible action—formulated as an action.

3. Arrange the possible actions into two categories:
   - Actions which others or 'the system' expect of you (pressure from system/others...)
   - Actions, which you yourself think/thought correct and would definitely have selected, if conditions permitted (I would like to...)

4. From the list, select the action for which there was the greatest pressure from others or 'the system'. Write this action in the field 'Pressure'.

5. Now write the course of action which is made impossible by this 'pressure' action (opposite action) in the 'Preferred' field. It may be the opposite of the action listed under 'Pressure', or it could be another action from the list, which with regards to content, is totally opposite to the pressure-action.

3.2.2 Example

Action	Pressure from system / others	I would like to...
I assert myself and we rent the apartment in X.		X
I give in, we rent the apartment in the neighboring village.	X	
We wait for a better offer.		X
We completely abandon the plan.	X	
We look in a different location.	X	
...		

Pressure	I give in, and we rent the apartment in the neighboring village.
Preferred	I assert myself and we rent the apartment in X.

3.2.3 My options for action

Action	Pressure from system / others	I would like to...

Pressure	
Preferred	

3.3. Create an Evaporating Cloud

Now you have prepared everything, you can create your first Evaporating Cloud from the template on the following page.

3.3.1 Instructions

1. Transfer the 'Pressure' action into field D.
2. Transfer the 'Preferred' action into field D'.
3. In box C write down the need that will be or should be satisfied by action D'.
4. Check the logic using the formula: (to achieve) C, I have to (ensure) D'.
5. In box B write down the need that will be or should be satisfied by action D.
6. Check the logic using the formula: (to achieve) B, I have to (ensure) D.
7. In field A, write down the common goal: Why are B and C so important? What achievements do B and C have in common? What are the prerequisites for both B and C? What is the common or ultimate goal?
8. Check the logic of the entire diagram using the formula:
   - In order (to achieve) A, I must (ensure) B.
   - In order (to achieve) B, I must (do) D.
   - In order (to achieve) A, I must (ensure) C.
   - In order (to achieve) C, I must (do) D'.
9. Adjust the formulations, so that they are 'coherent' and represent the problem or dilemma clearly.
10. Finally, carry out cross-matching. The action in D endangers need C, conversely, act D' endangers need B. Endangered in this respect means the likelihood of satisfying the need on the other branch, significantly decreases, even if it is possible to achieve it under certain circumstances.

3.3.2 Example

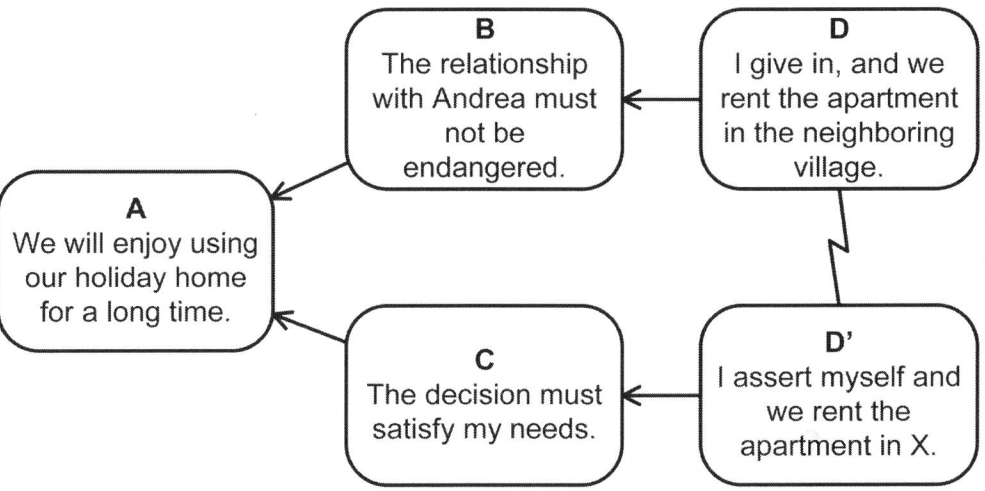

Review of the formulation:

- In order that (A) we enjoy our apartment for a long time, I must ensure that (B) the relationship with Andrea is not endangered.
- To achieve a situation where (B) the relationship with Andrea is not endangered, I need to (D) give in and we rent the apartment in the neighboring village.
- In order that (A) we enjoy our apartment for a long time, the decision must (C) satisfy my needs.
- In order that (C) the decision satisfies my needs, I must (D') assert myself and we rent the apartment in X.
- If (D) I give in, and we rent the apartment in the neighboring village, essentially my needs will not be met (C).
- If (D') I assert myself, and we rent the apartment in X, then the relationship with Andrea will deteriorate.

3.3.3 My dilemma—1. outline

Note: You will probably end up revising your formulations several times. Therefore, it might be a good idea to use sticky notes initially, instead of writing directly on the paper. Alternatively, you can revise your formulations on the following pages.

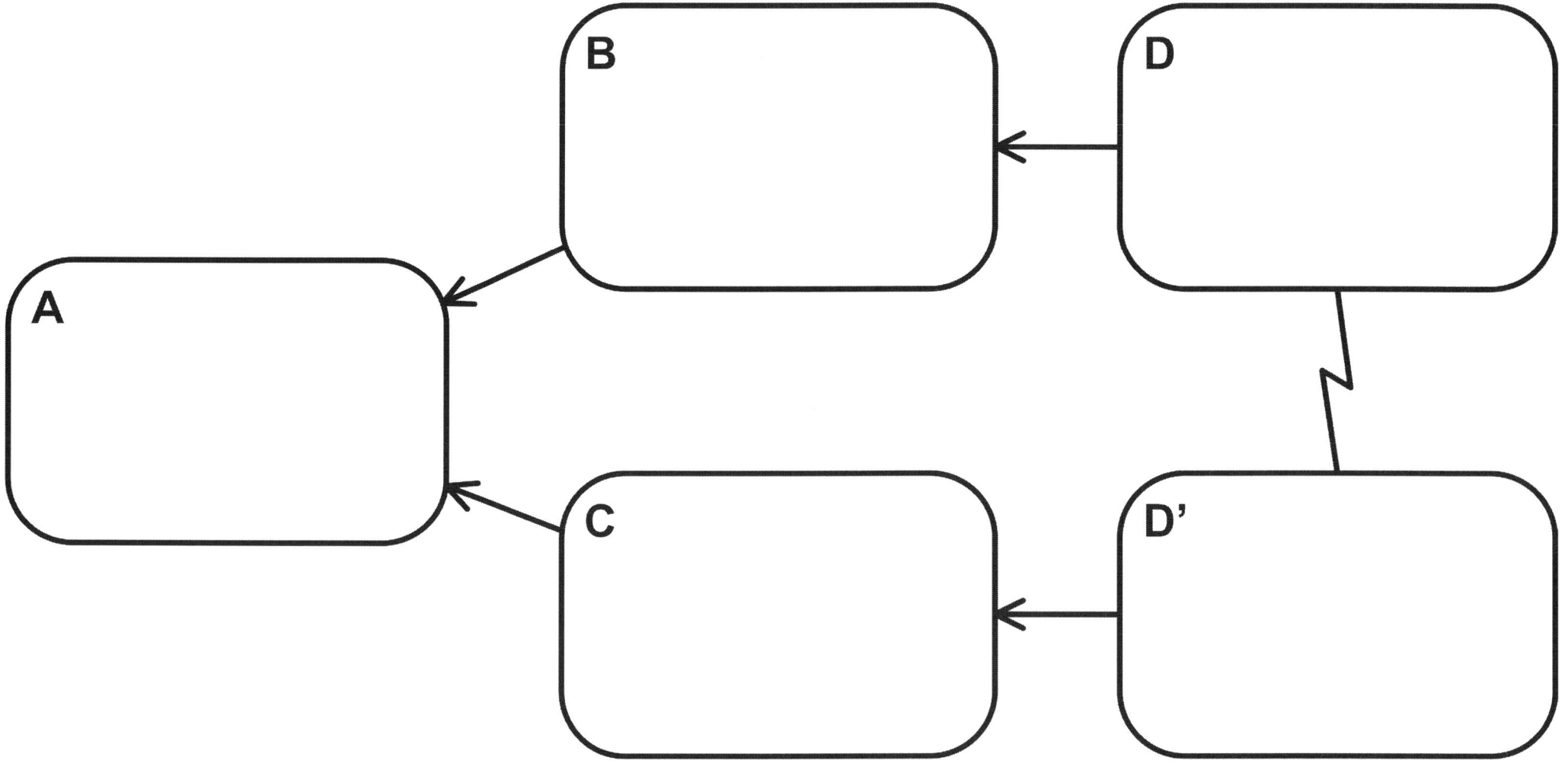

3.3.4 My dilemma — 2. outline

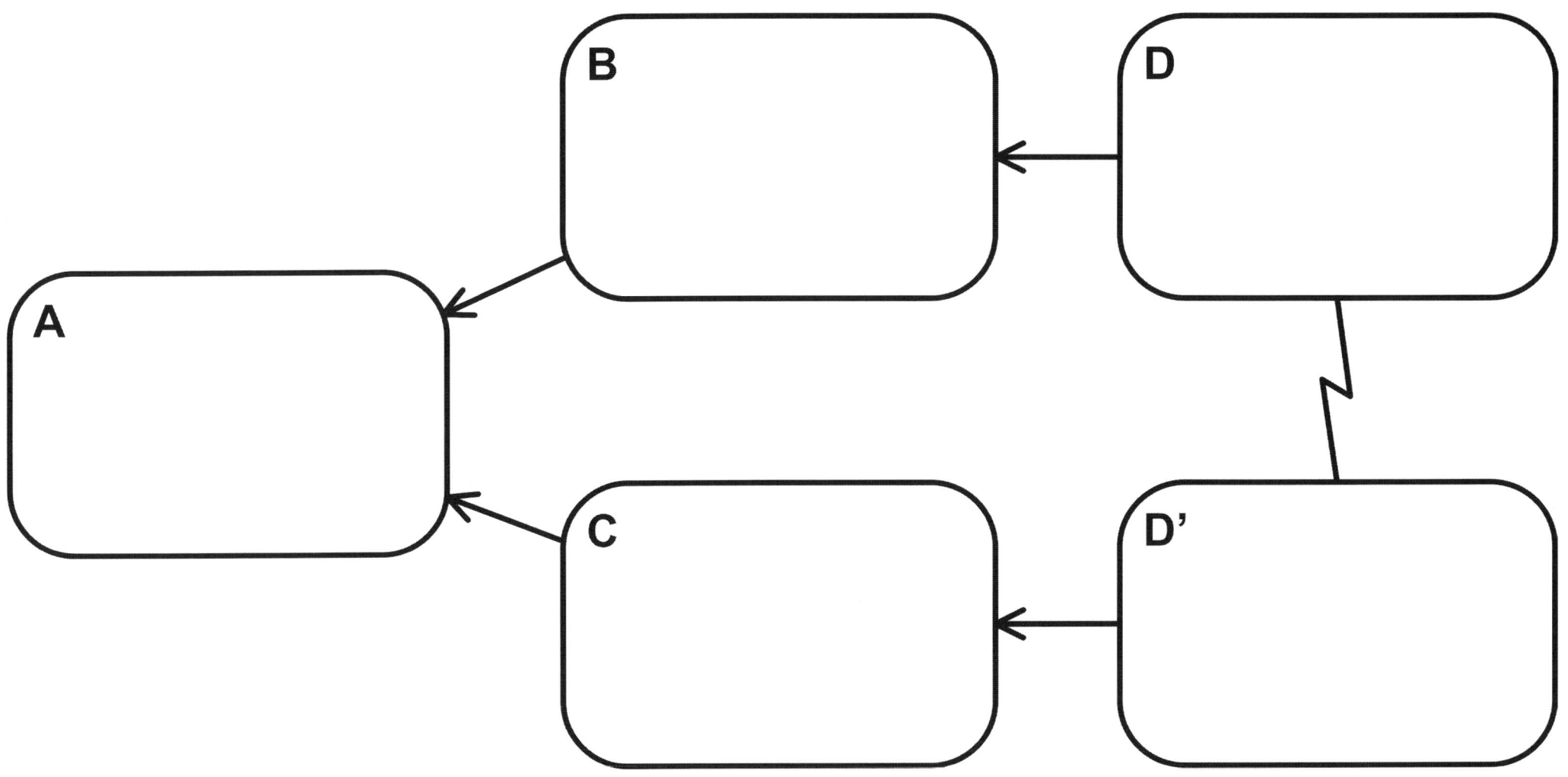

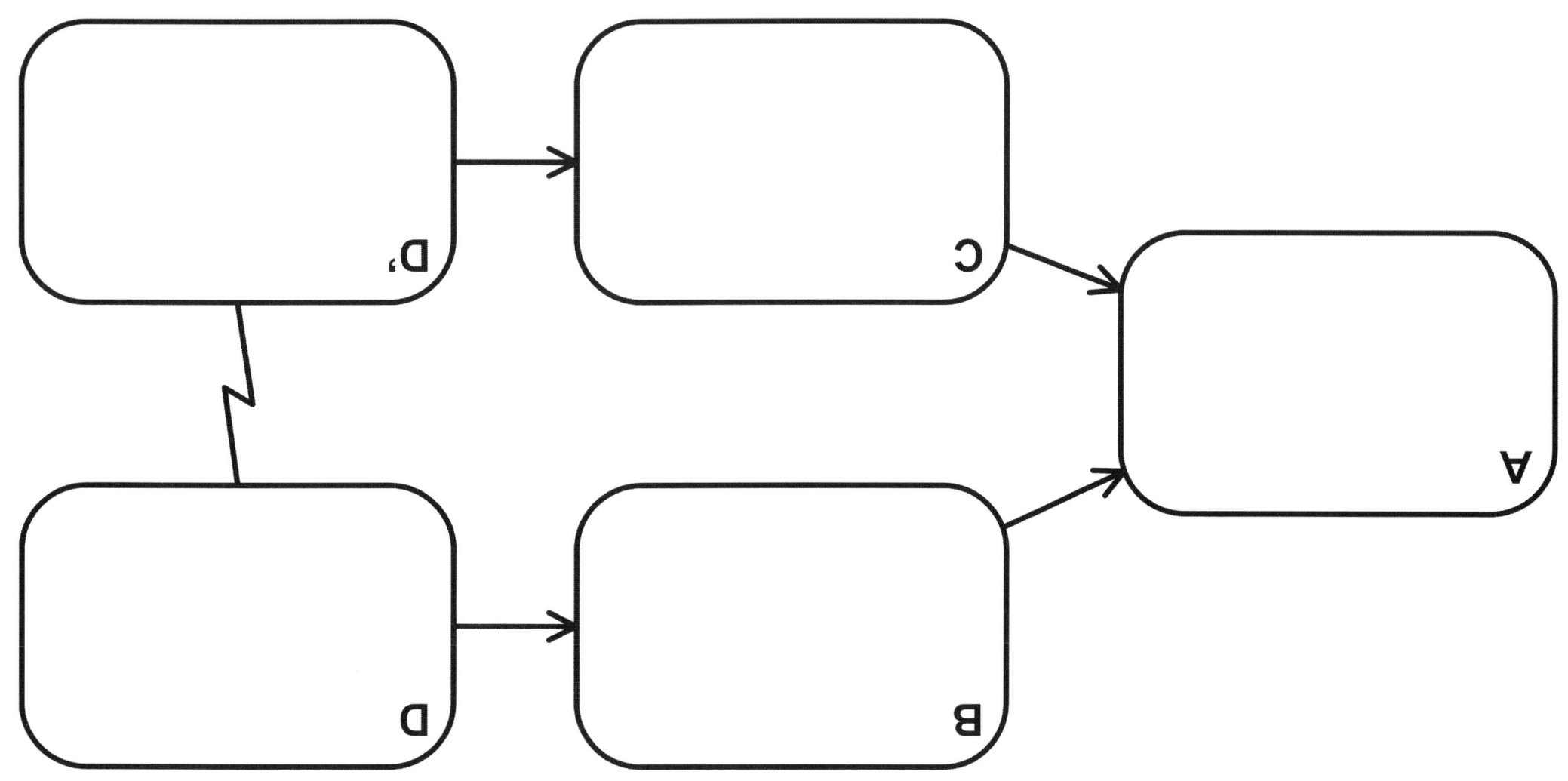

3.3.5 My dilemma – 3. outline

3.4 Assumptions

3.4.1 Instructions

There are good reasons for carrying out D in order to achieve B. There are also good reasons for carrying out D' in order to achieve C. These reasons are stored as assumptions in our thoughts, but often not spoken out loud. In order to consider them and understand them more accurately, we will write them down. The assumptions need to explain the relationship between the elements and not just be reformulated in other words. The more assumptions you can find, the better; assumptions are a valuable source of possible solutions.

1. Make a note of the reasons why D has to be carried out in order to achieve B. To do this, complete this sentence: 'To achieve B, I need to do D, because...' This formulates why B can only be achieved through action D. Find at least three, preferably five such reasons.

2. Repeat this step for the relationship between D' and C, B and A, as well as between C and A.

3. Write down reasons, why it is a dilemma at all, and why the problem is not solvable for you. Why are D and D' mutually exclusive? Find at least three, preferably five such reasons.

3.4.2 Example

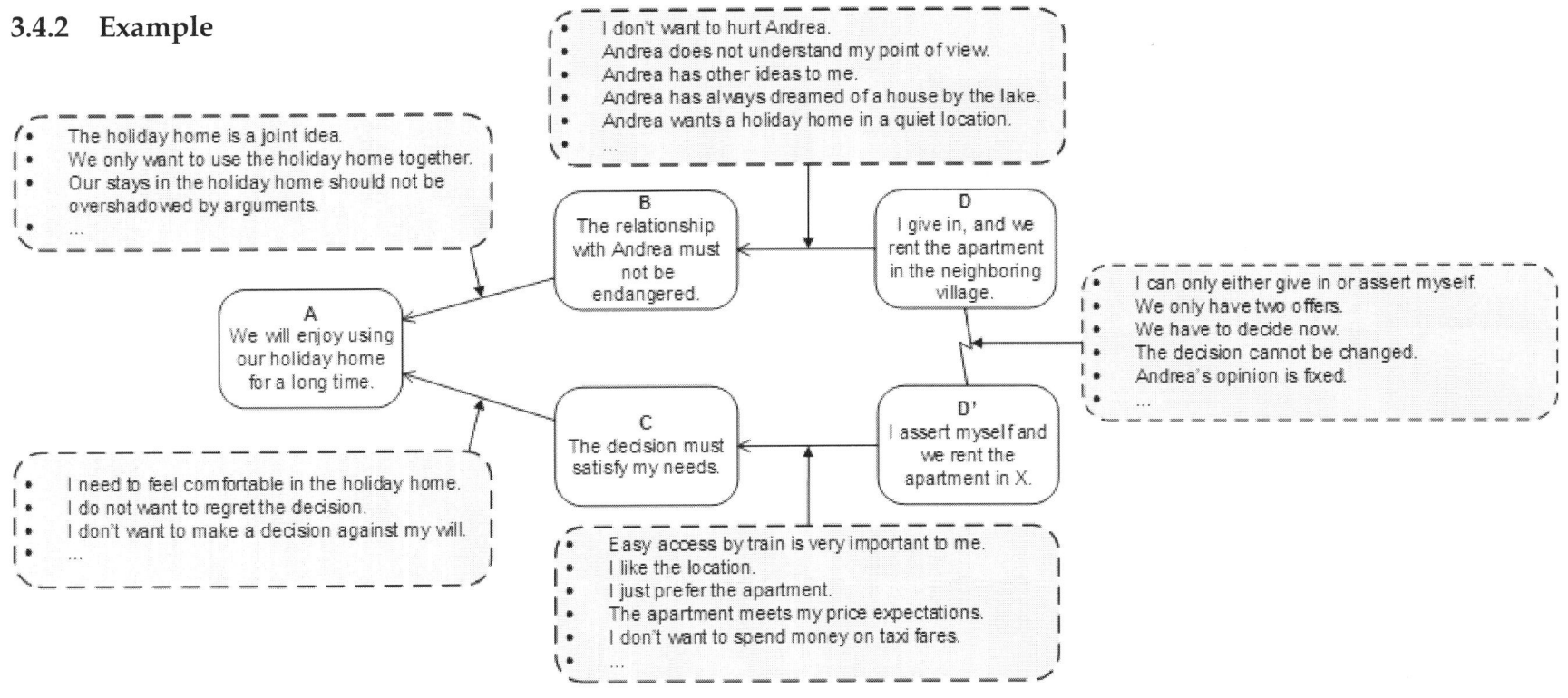

Workbook Win-Win Solutions

3.4.3 My dilemma with assumptions — 1. outline

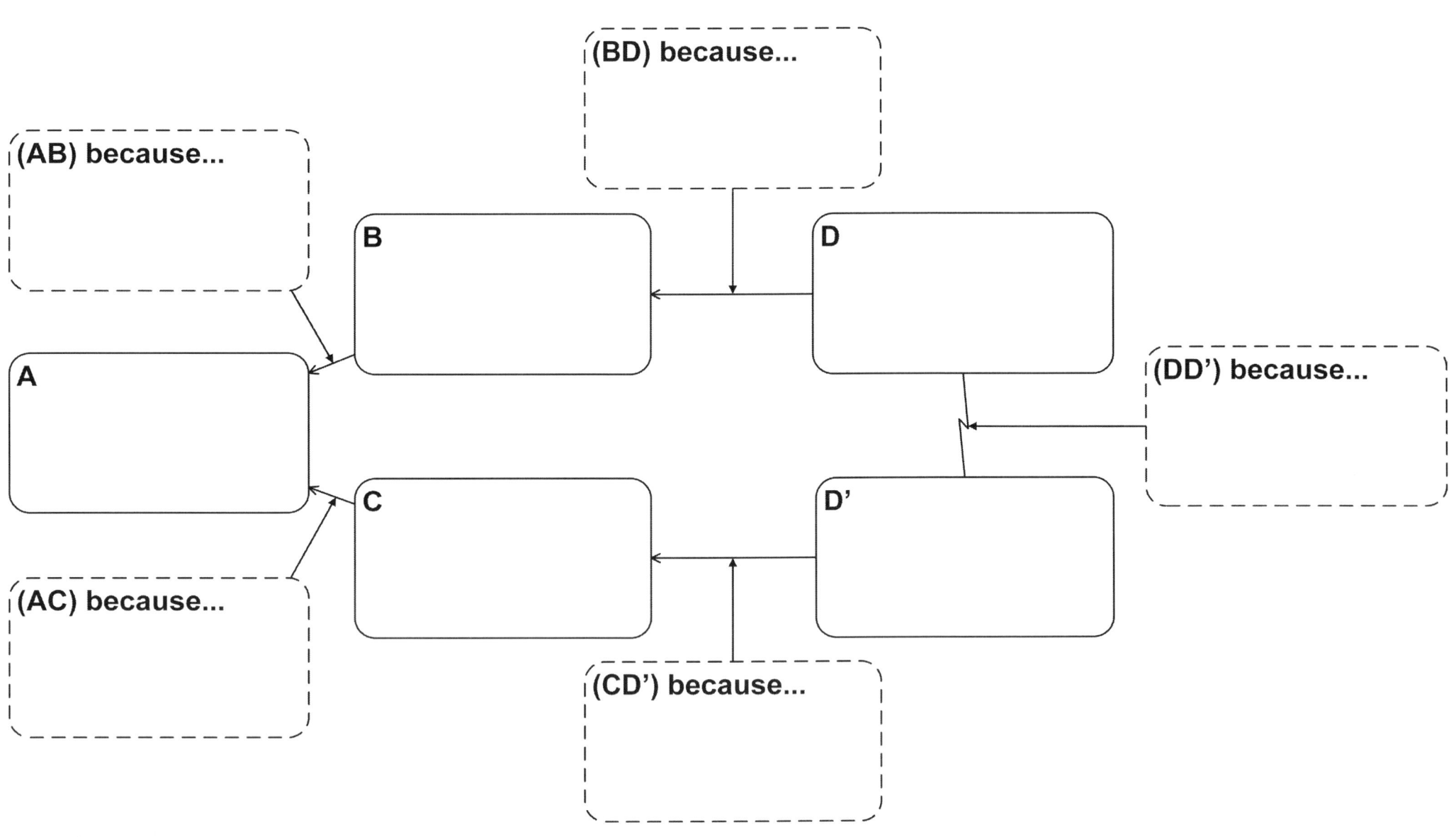

3.4.4 My dilemma with assumptions — 2. outline

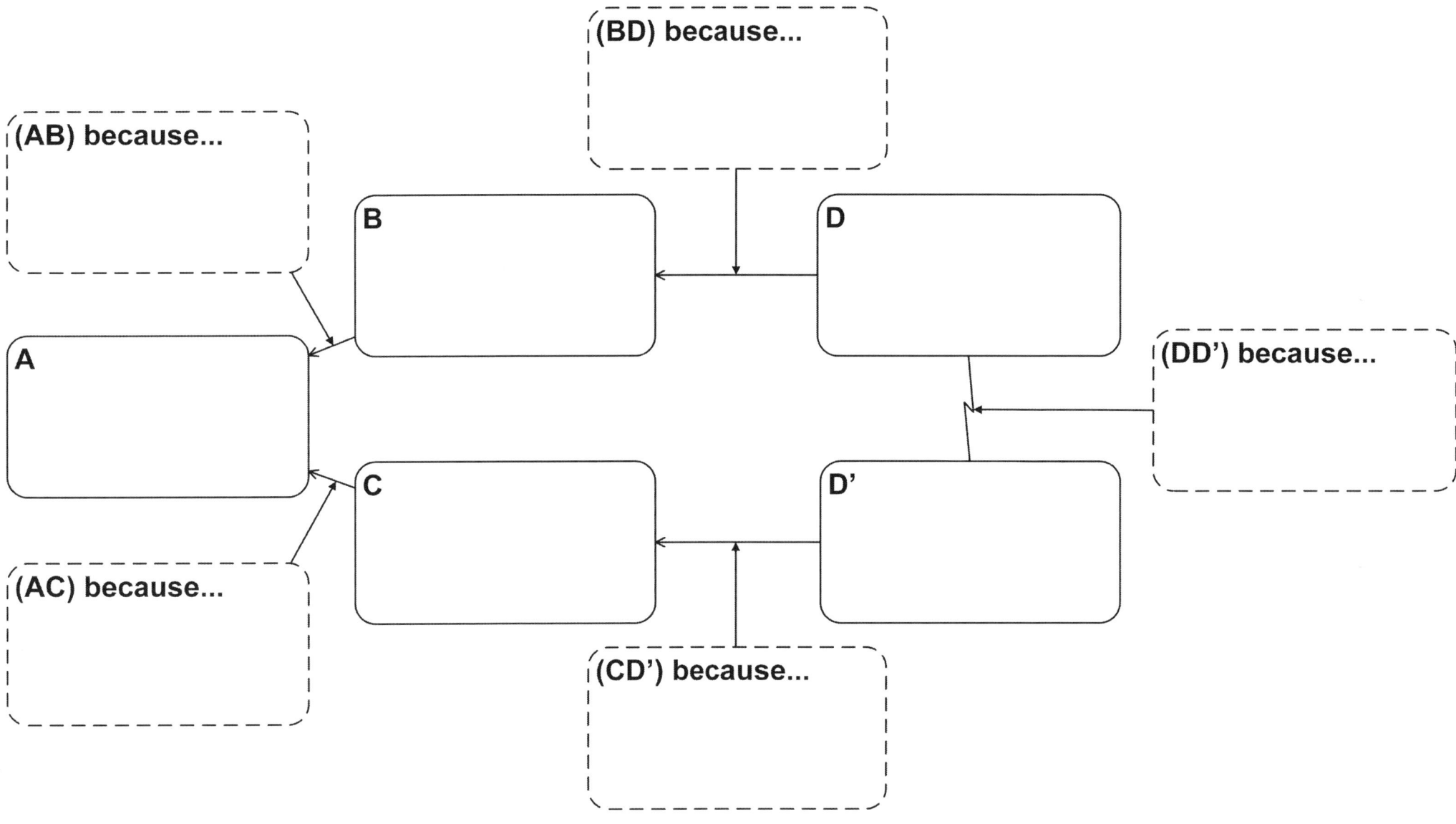

Dilemma 21

3.5 Develop possible solutions

Assumptions are the very reason that a dilemma exists at all. If there is a way to resolve or convert the reasons for the dilemma, the problem will resolve itself. To successfully do this, we need to find a new assumption and integrate it into the system.

3.5.1 Instructions

1. Transfer the two strongest assumptions for A-C, A-B, B-D, C-D', D-D ' into the overview on the next page.

2. Write down the possibilities that could follow, if the reasons or assumptions were eliminated or converted.

   Tips:

   - Search for flawed (or very weak) assumptions ('actually that can't be...').
   - Formulate assumptions in absolute terms ('There is no other way, than...').
   - Which assumptions contradict fundamental system objectives ('we can't have such a thing...')?
   - Search for a reference environment in which the assumption is not required ('under these conditions the assumption is superfluous...').
   - Do not discard any ideas or solutions, because they appear too difficult ('castles in the air' or 'pigs can fly'), or because you have already tried them out ('you can't, do that as we have already tried that out, we don't want that...').

3. Starting points:

   - A breakthrough solution may apply to any of the prerequisite relationships (A-C, A-B, B-D, C-D') but also to the conflict itself (D-D').
   - You should first examine B-D, C-D' and D-D'.

3.5.2 Example

	Reasons / assumptions	Possible solutions
A-B	• We only want to use the holiday home together. • Our stays in the holiday home should not be overshadowed by arguments.	• We have a holiday home in which we spend short and long vacations together without arguing.
A-C	• I do not want to regret the decision. • I don't want to make any decisions against my will.	• The decision takes into account my needs and expectations.
B-D	• I don't want to hurt Andrea. • Andrea does not understand my point of view.	• I'll demonstrate to Andrea that I take her views seriously and explain my needs and expectations, without hurting her.
C-D'	• Easy access by train is very important to me. • The apartment meets my price expectations.	• The holiday home is quick and easy to reach. • We have so much money, that the price doesn't matter.
D-D'	• The decision is unchangeable. • Andrea's opinion is fixed.	• We can 'test' a holiday home. • We will find a solution that we both fully agree to.

3.5.3 My possible solutions

	Reasons / assumptions	Possible solutions
A-B		
A-C		
B-D		
C-D'		
D-D'		

3.6 Solution

3.6.1 Instructions

In the following, we assume that you have applied your solution to one of the assumptions B-D or C-D'.

1. Transfer A, B and C from the original Evaporating Cloud into the solution template.
2. Select a solution (or a combination) from the list of Possible Solutions, and transfer it into the 'Possible Solutions' box.
3. Check to see that the solution meets the needs of B and C: 'If I carry out/ensure the solution activity then I will attain B and C, because...'.
4. Include reasons why the solution leads to satisfying the needs of B and C.
5. If the solution and the two reasons are inconsistent, work on the formulation or select another option from the list of possible solutions.
6. Check to see whether you would actually feel better if it were to happen.

3.6.2 Example

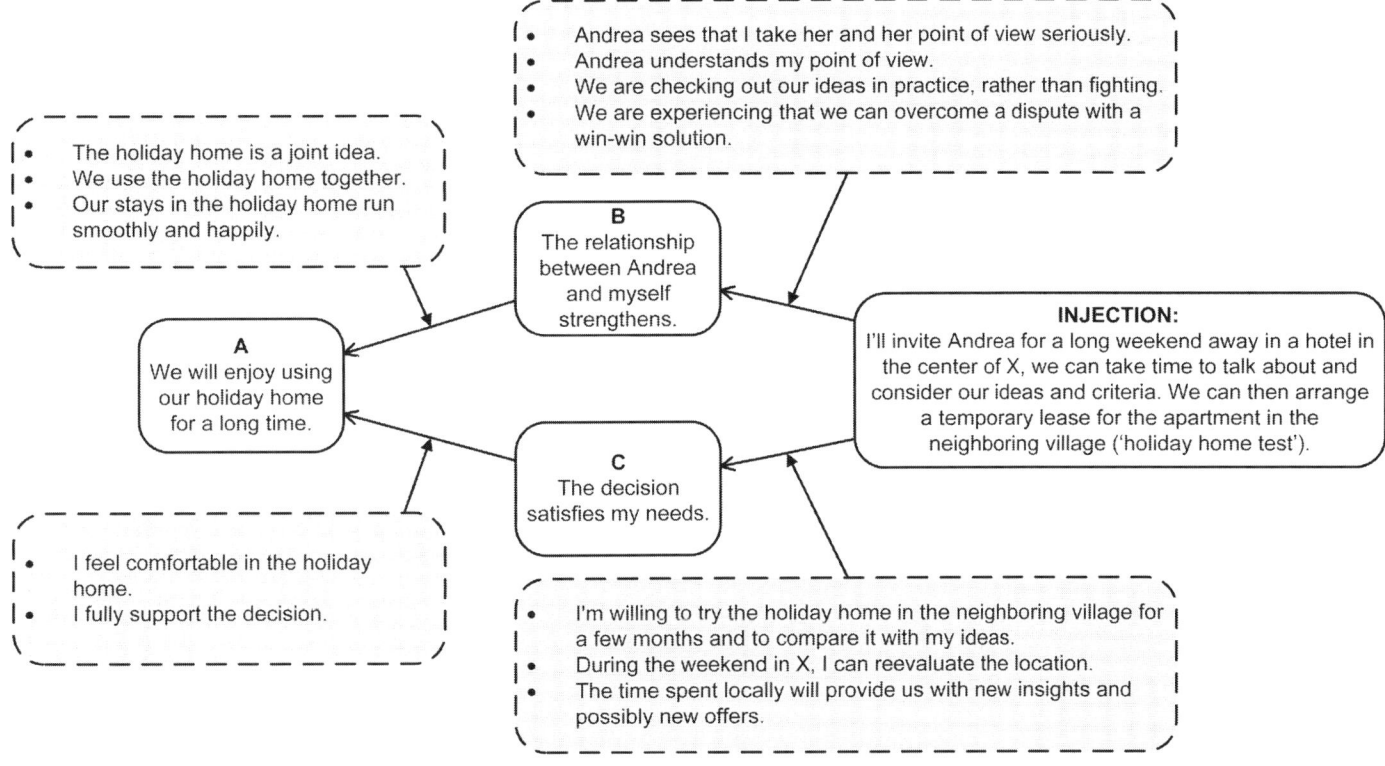

Workbook Win-Win Solutions

3.6.3 My solution (1. outline)

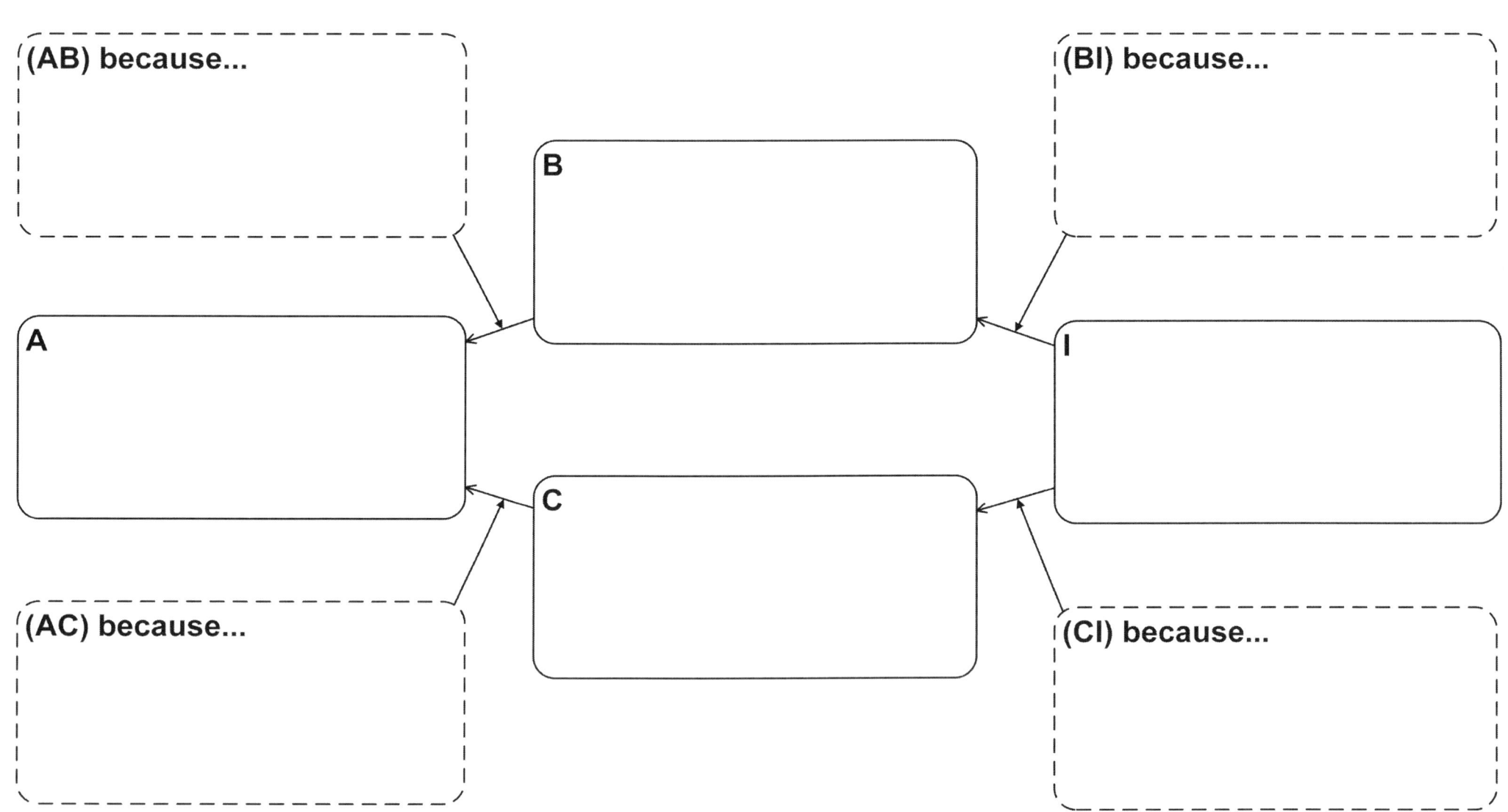

3.6.4 My solution (2. outline)

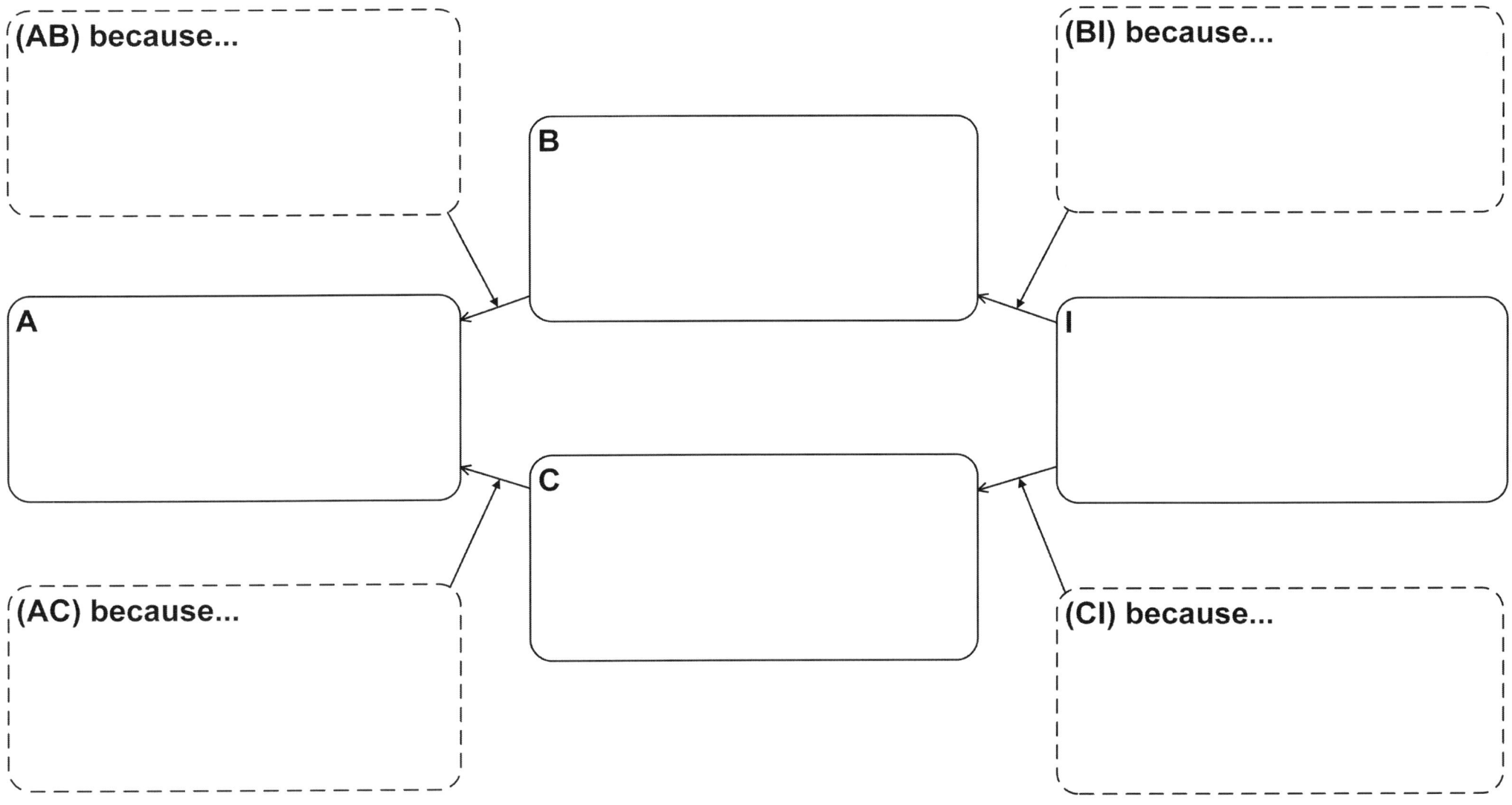

4 Dilemma — exercise 2 (with full instructions)

4.1 Problem report

4.1.1 Instructions

Write a report on your problem — as if you were writing an essay or a letter of complaint. In the report, explain why this situation presents a problem, and how you and your services will be/were affected.

Take into account the following questions:

- Who are the participants?
- What happened?
- When, and in what context did the situation occur?
- Where did it happen?
- What did I want to do? Why?
- What should I not do? Why?

The purpose of the Problem Report is to help you to put the facts, and your thoughts on the selected problem, down on paper, so they can be subsequently processed and structured.

4.1.2 Example

Title / topic	Andrea and I want to rent a holiday home in X and we are unable to choose between offers.
Report	Andrea and I have been looking for a holiday home for a long time, and now we have two interesting offers. On the one hand, a one bedroom apartment in X, and on the other a larger two bedroom apartment in the neighboring village with a lake view. The apartment in X is located in the town center with restaurants and shops, a few minutes walk from the train station, and it would be possible to arrive by train every hour until one o'clock in the morning. I also find the price quite reasonable. We can only reach the neighboring village by means of an inconvenient bus connection or taxi. Andrea is worried, however, that it might be a tight squeeze in a one-bedroom apartment. Therefore, she prefers the location on the outskirts by the lake in the neighboring village, where she believes she will be able to relax better. Of course, we could decide on neither and wait for an even better deal. Recently we have fought a few times on this issue and I'm worried that our relationship could really suffer. Now, I don't know what action to take.

Workbook Win-Win Solutions

4.1.3 My problem report

Title / topic	
Report	

4.2 Possible actions

4.2.1 Instructions

1. Create a list of possible actions.

2. Consider:
   - Actions which you think or would have thought are right.
   - Actions which others or 'the system' expect of you.

3. Write a short, clear sentence for each possible action—formulated as an action.

4. Arrange the possible actions into two categories:
   - Actions which others or 'the system' expect of you (pressure from system/others...)
   - Actions, which you yourself think/thought correct and would definitely have selected, if conditions permitted (I would like to...)

5. From the list, select the action for which there was the greatest pressure from others or 'the system'. Write this action in the field 'Pressure'.

6. Now write the course of action which is made impossible by this 'pressure' action (opposite action) in the 'Preferred' field. It may be the opposite of the action listed under 'Pressure', or it could be another action from the list, which with regards to content, is totally opposite to the pressure-action.

4.2.2 Example

Action	Pressure from system / others	I would like to...
I assert myself and we rent the apartment in X.		X
I give in, we rent the apartment in the neighboring village.	X	
We wait for a better offer.		X
We completely abandon the plan.	X	
We look in a different location.	X	
...		

Pressure	I give in, and we rent the apartment in the neighboring village.
Preferred	I assert myself and we rent the apartment in X.

4.2.3 My options for action

Action	Pressure from system / others	I would like to...

Pressure	
Preferred	

4.3 Create an Evaporating Cloud

Create an Evaporating Cloud from the template on the following page.

4.3.1 Instructions

1. Transfer the 'Pressure' action into field D.

2. Transfer the 'Preferred' action into field D'.

3. In box C write down the need that will be or should be satisfied by action D'.

4. Check the logic using the formula: (to achieve) C, I have to (ensure) D.

5. In box B write down the need that will be or should be satisfied by action D.

6. Check the logic using the formula: (to achieve) B, I have to (ensure) D.

7. In field A, write down the common goal: Why are B and C so important? What achievements do B and C have in common? What are prerequisites for both B and C ? What is the common or ultimate goal?

8. Check the logic of the entire diagram using the formula:
   - In order (to achieve) A, I must (ensure) B.
   - In order (to achieve) B, I must (do) D.
   - In order (to achieve) A, I must (ensure) C.
   - In order (to achieve) C, I must (do) D'.

9. Adjust the formulations, so that they are 'coherent' and represent the problem or dilemma clearly.

10. Finally, carry out cross-matching. Action D endangers need C, conversely action D' endangers need B. Endangered in this respect means the likelihood of satisfying the need on the other branch significantly decreases, even if it is possible to achieve it under certain circumstances.

4.3.2 Example

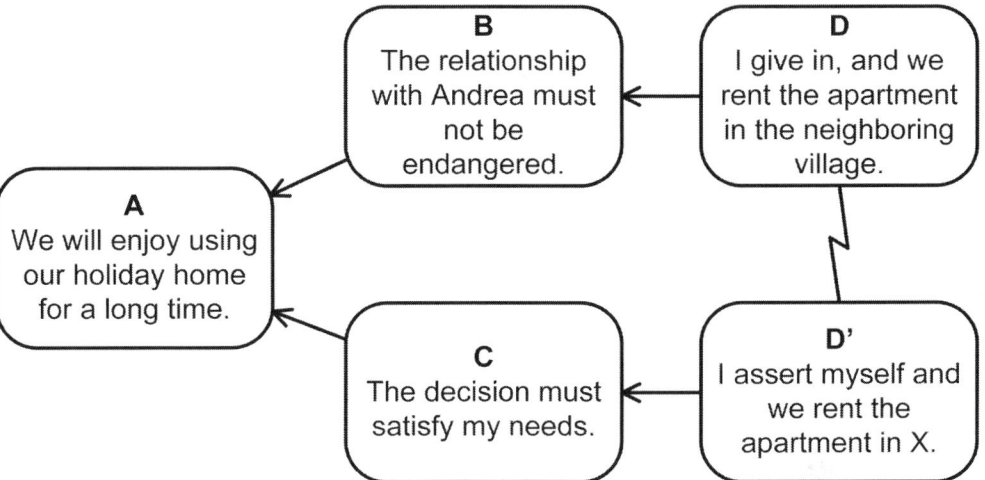

Review of the formulation:
- In order that (A) we enjoy using our holiday home for a long time, I need to ensure that (B) the relationship with Andrea is not endangered.
- To ensure that (B) the relationship with Andrea is not endangered, I need to (D) give in, and we rent the apartment in the neighboring village.
- In order that (A) we enjoy using our holiday home for a long time, the decision must (C) satisfy my needs.
- In order that (C) the decision satisfies my needs, I need to (D') assert myself and we rent the apartment in X.
- If (D) I give in, and we rent the apartment in the neighboring village, essentially, my needs will not be met (C).
- If (D') I assert myself and we rent the apartment in X, then the relationship with Andrea will suffer.

4.3.3 My dilemma — 1. outline

Note: You will probably end up revising your formulations several times. Therefore, it might be a good idea to use sticky notes initially, instead of writing directly on the paper. Alternatively, you can revise your formulations on the following pages.

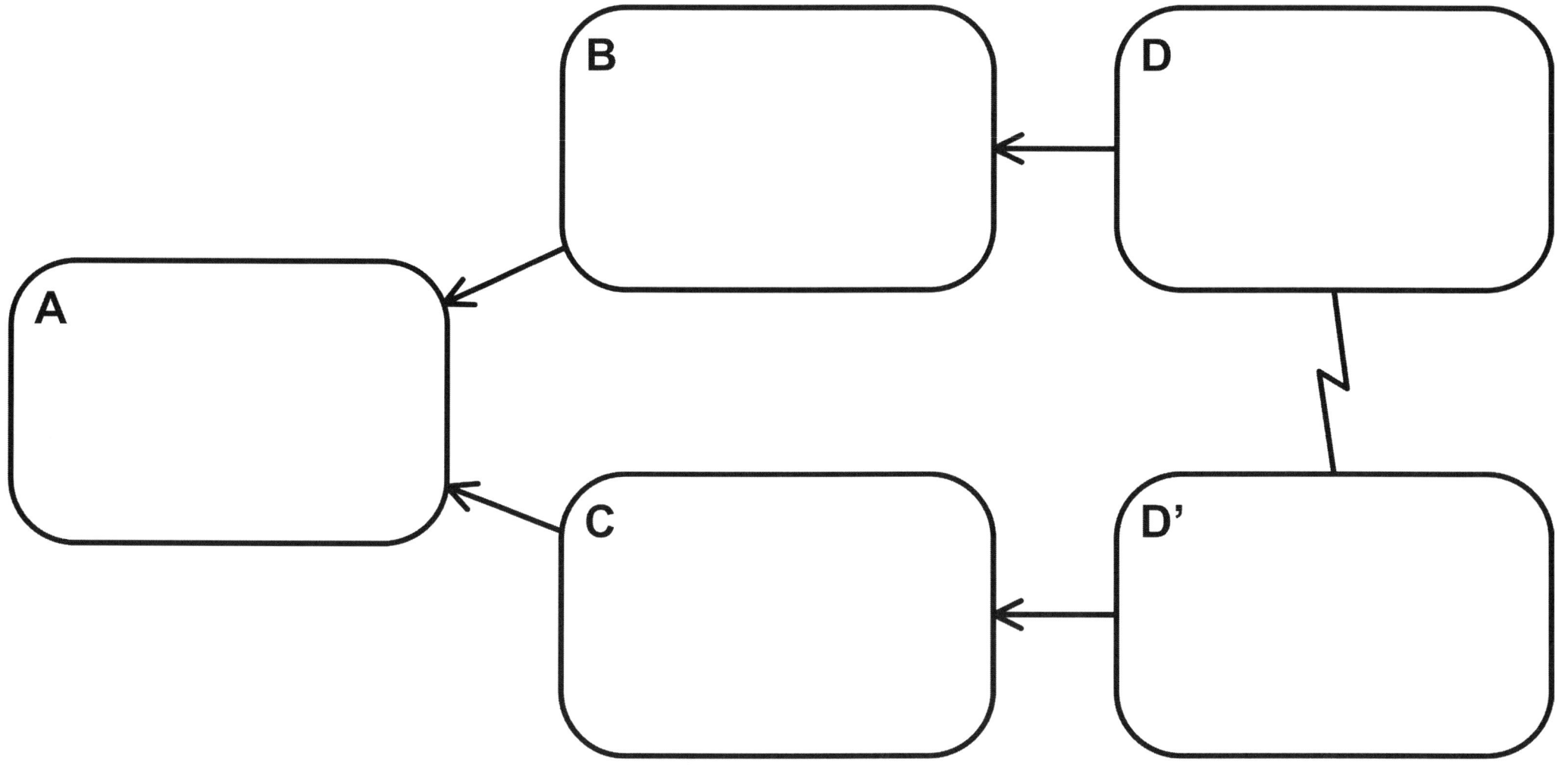

4.3.4 My dilemma — 2. outline

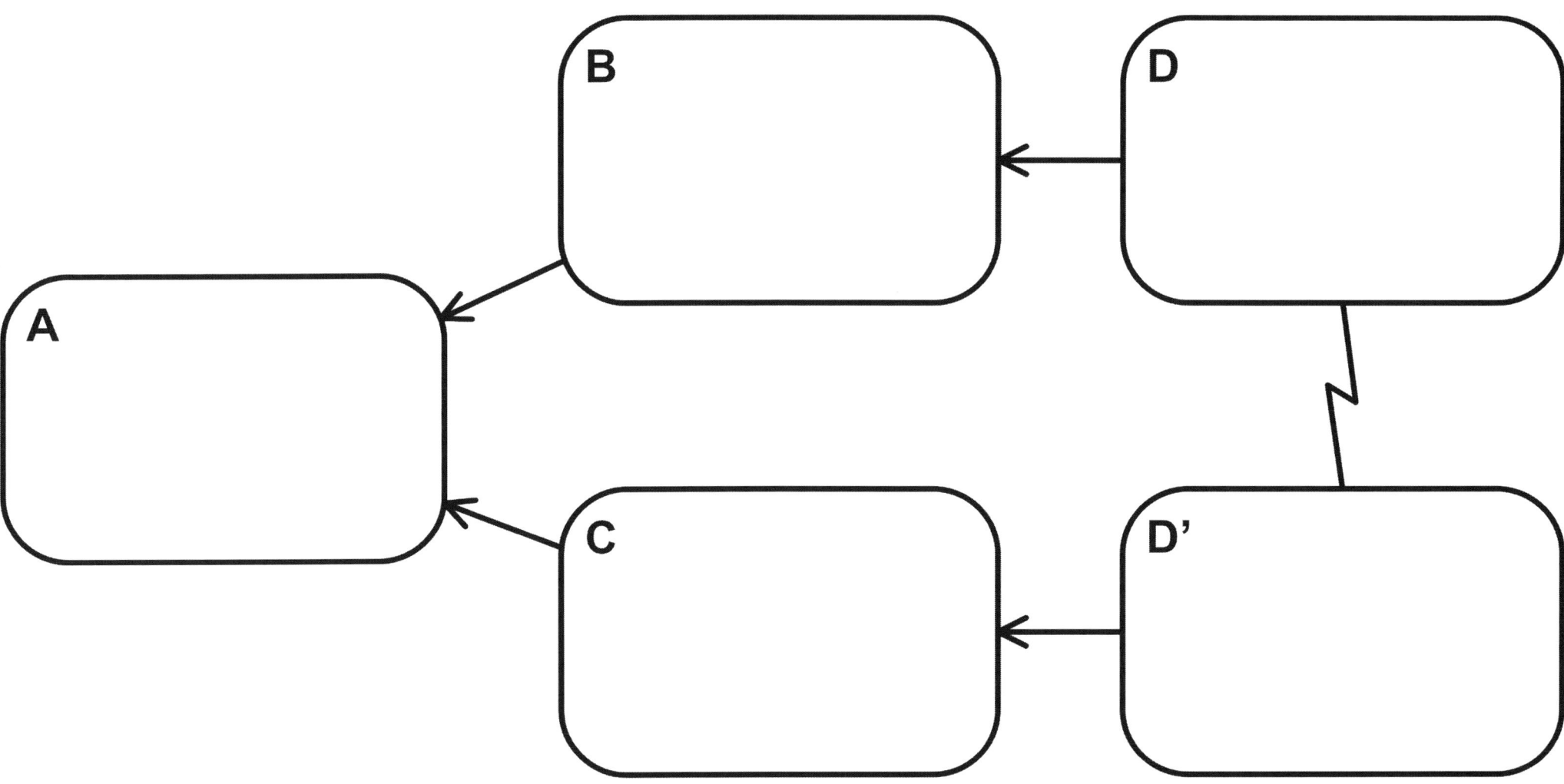

Dilemma

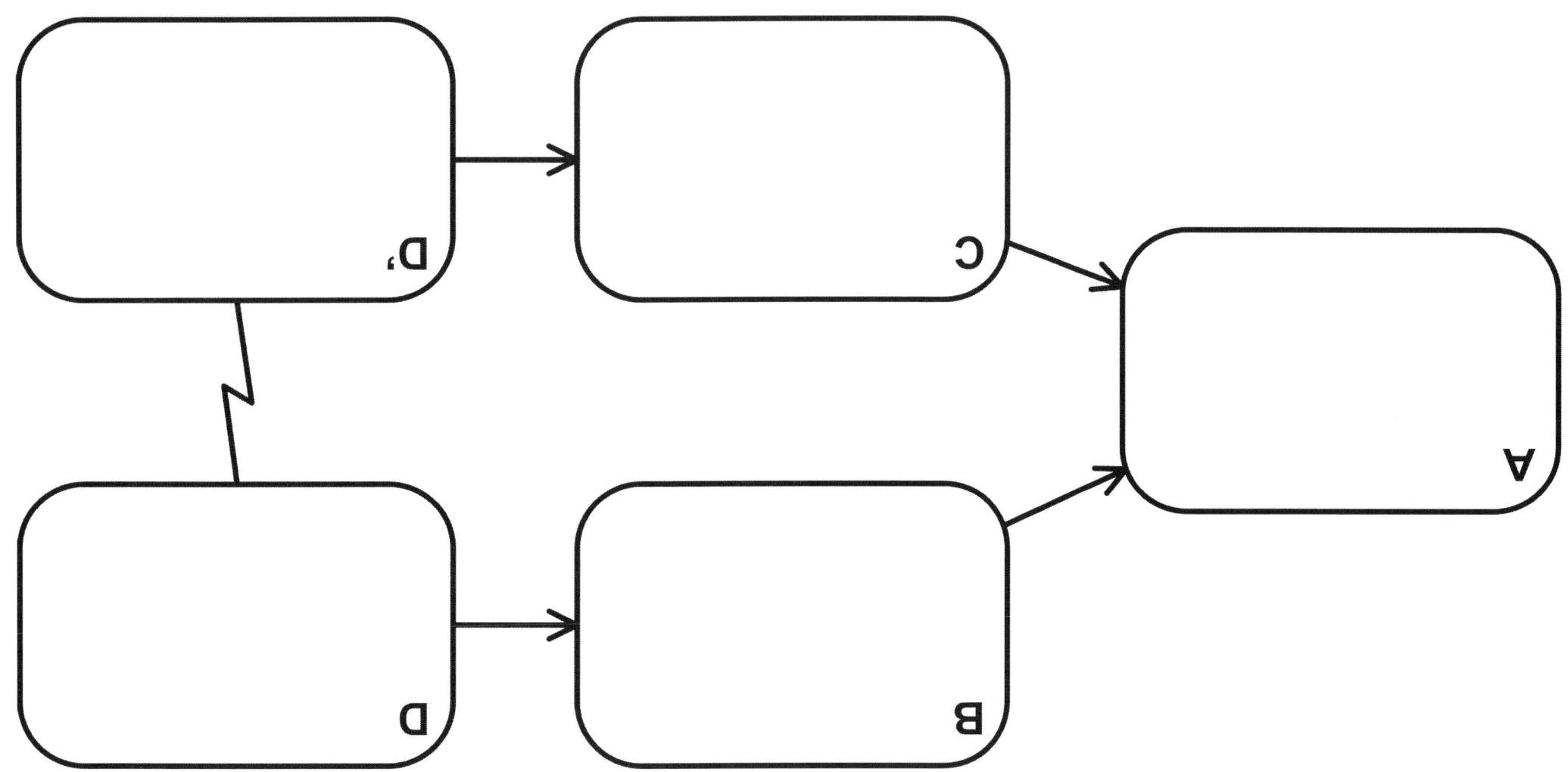

4.3.5 My dilemma – 3. outline

4.4 Assumptions

4.4.1 Instructions

There are good reasons for carrying out D in order to achieve B. There are also good reasons for carrying out D' in order to achieve C. These reasons are stored as assumptions in our thoughts, but often not spoken out loud. In order to consider them and understand them more accurately, we will now write them down.

The assumptions need to explain the relationship between the elements and not just be reformulated in other words. The more assumptions you can find, the better; assumptions are a valuable source of possible solutions.

1. Make a note of the reasons why D has to be carried out in order to achieve B. To do this, complete this sentence: 'To achieve B, I need to do D, because...'. This formulates why B can only be achieved through action D. Find at least three, preferably five such reasons.
2. Repeat this step for the relationship between D' and C, between B and A, as well as between C and A.
3. Write down reasons, why it is a dilemma at all, and why the problem is not solvable for you. Why are D and D' mutually exclusive? Find at least three, preferably five such reasons.

4.4.2 Example

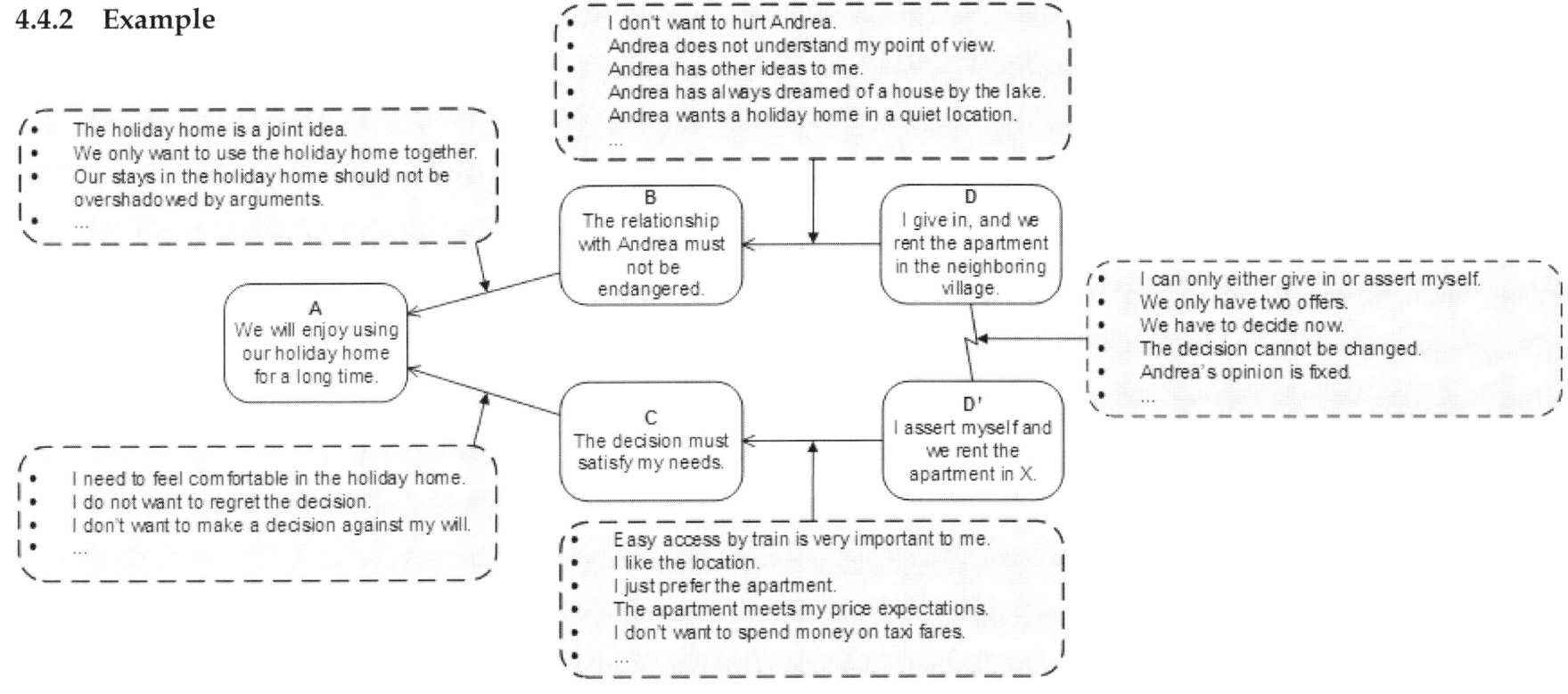

4.4.3 My dilemma with assumptions — 1. outline

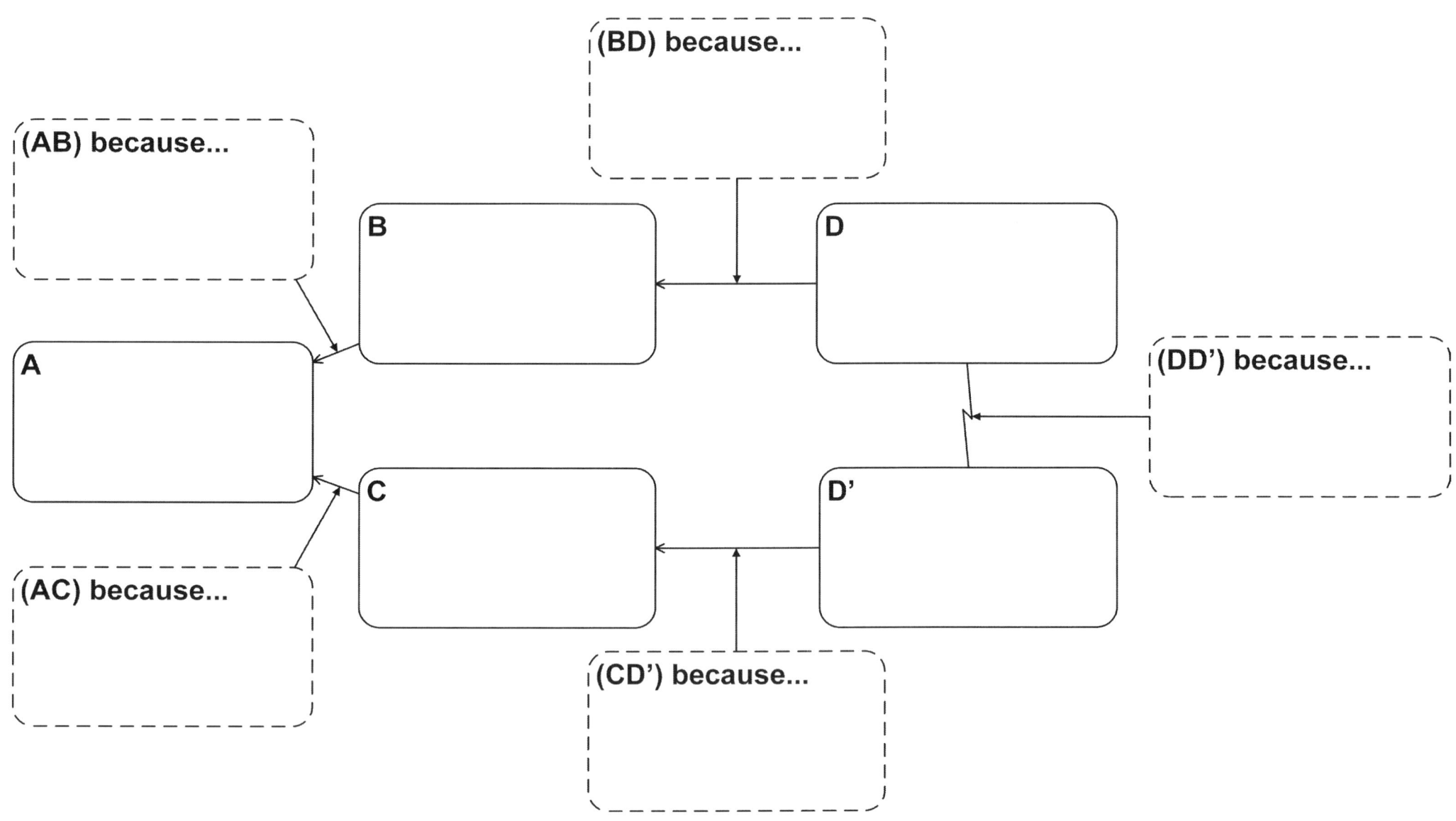

4.4.4 My dilemma with assumptions — 2. outline

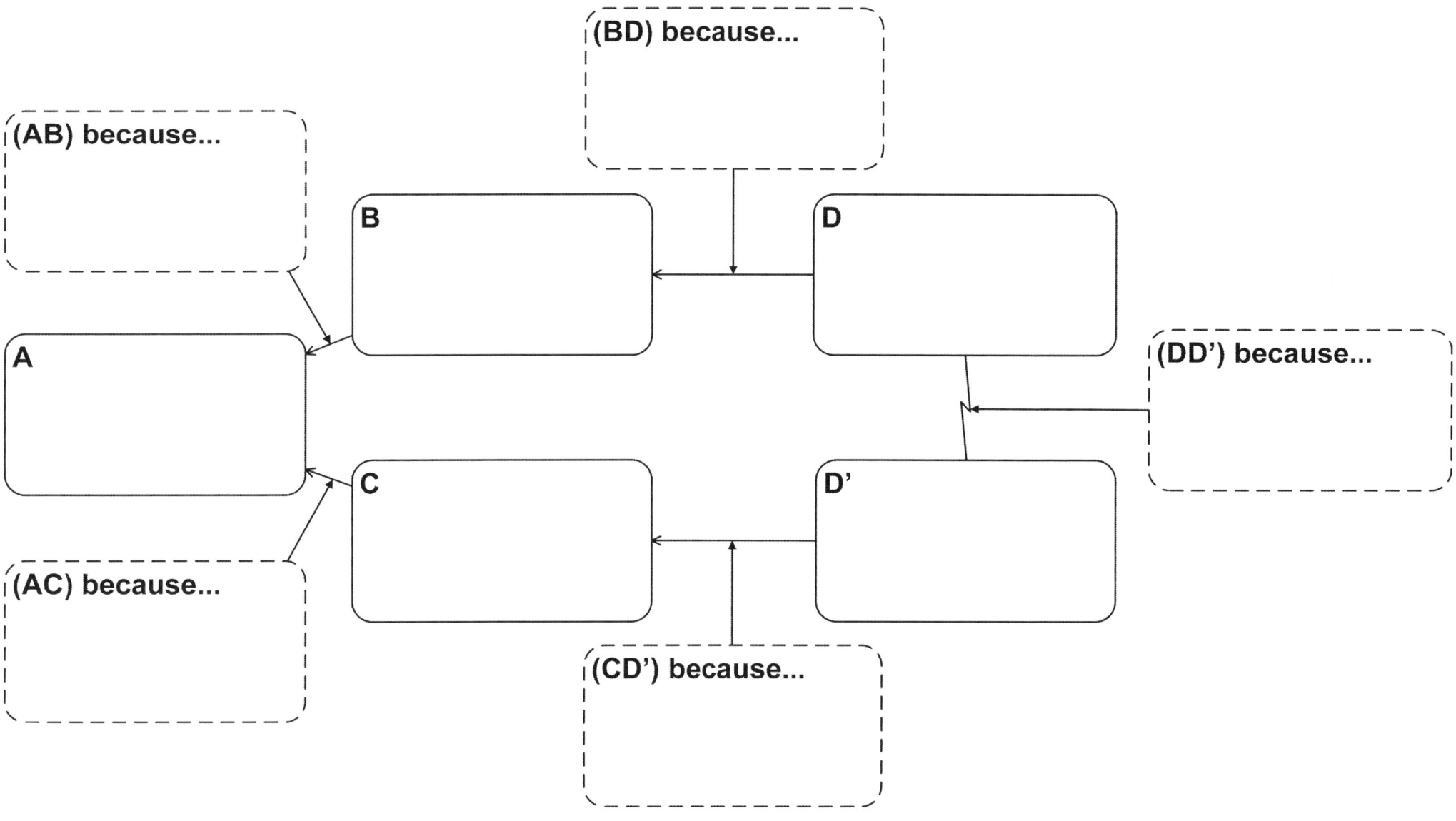

Dilemma

4.5 Develop possible solutions

Assumptions are the very reason that a dilemma exists at all. If there is a way to resolve or convert the reasons for the dilemma, the problem will resolve itself. To successfully do this, we need to find a new assumption and integrate it into the system.

4.5.1 Instructions

1. Transfer the two strongest assumptions for A-C, A-B, B-D, C-D', D-D ' into the overview on the next page.

2. Write down the possibilities that could follow, if the reasons or assumptions were eliminated or converted.

   Tips:

   - Search for flawed (or very weak) assumptions ('actually that can't be...').
   - Formulate assumptions in absolute terms ('There is no other way, than...').
   - Which assumptions contradict fundamental system objectives ('we can't have such a thing...')?
   - Search for a reference environment in which the assumption is not required ('under these conditions the assumption is superfluous...').
   - Do not discard any ideas or solutions, because they appear too difficult ('castles in the air' or 'pigs can fly'), or because you have already tried them out ('you can't, do that as we have already tried that out, we don't want that...').

3. Starting points:

   - A breakthrough solution may apply to any of the prerequisite relationships (A-C, A-B, B-D, C-D') but also to the conflict itself (D-D').
   - You should first examine B-D, C-D' and D-D'.

4.5.2 Example

	Reasons / assumptions	Possible solutions
A-B	- We only want to use the holiday home together. - Our stays in the holiday home should not be overshadowed by arguments.	- We have a holiday home in which we spend short and long vacations together without arguing.
A-C	- I do not want to regret the decision. - I don't want to make any decisions against my will.	- The decision takes into account my needs and expectations.
B-D	- I don't want to hurt Andrea. - Andrea does not understand my point of view.	- I'll demonstrate to Andrea that I take her views seriously and explain my needs and expectations, without hurting her.
C-D'	- Easy access by train is very important to me. - The apartment meets my price expectations.	- The holiday home is quick and easy to reach. - We have so much money, that the price doesn't matter.
D-D'	- The decision is unchangeable. - Andrea's opinion is fixed.	- We can 'test' a holiday home. - We will find a solution that we both fully agree to.

4.5.3 My possible solutions

	Reasons / assumptions	Possible solutions
A-B		
A-C		
B-D		
C-D'		
D-D'		

4.6 Solution

4.6.1 Instructions

In the following, we assume that you have applied your solution to one of the assumptions B-D or C-D'.

1. Transfer A, B and C from the original Evaporating Cloud into the solution template.
2. Select a solution (or a combination) from the list of Possible Solutions, and transfer it into the 'Possible Solutions' box.
3. Check to see that the solution meets the needs of B and C: 'If I carry out/ensure the solution activity then I will attain B and C, because...'.
4. Include reasons why the solution leads to satisfying the needs of B and C.
5. If the solution and the two reasons are inconsistent, work on the formulation or select another option from the list of possible solutions.
6. Check to see whether you would actually feel better if it were to happen.

4.6.2 Example

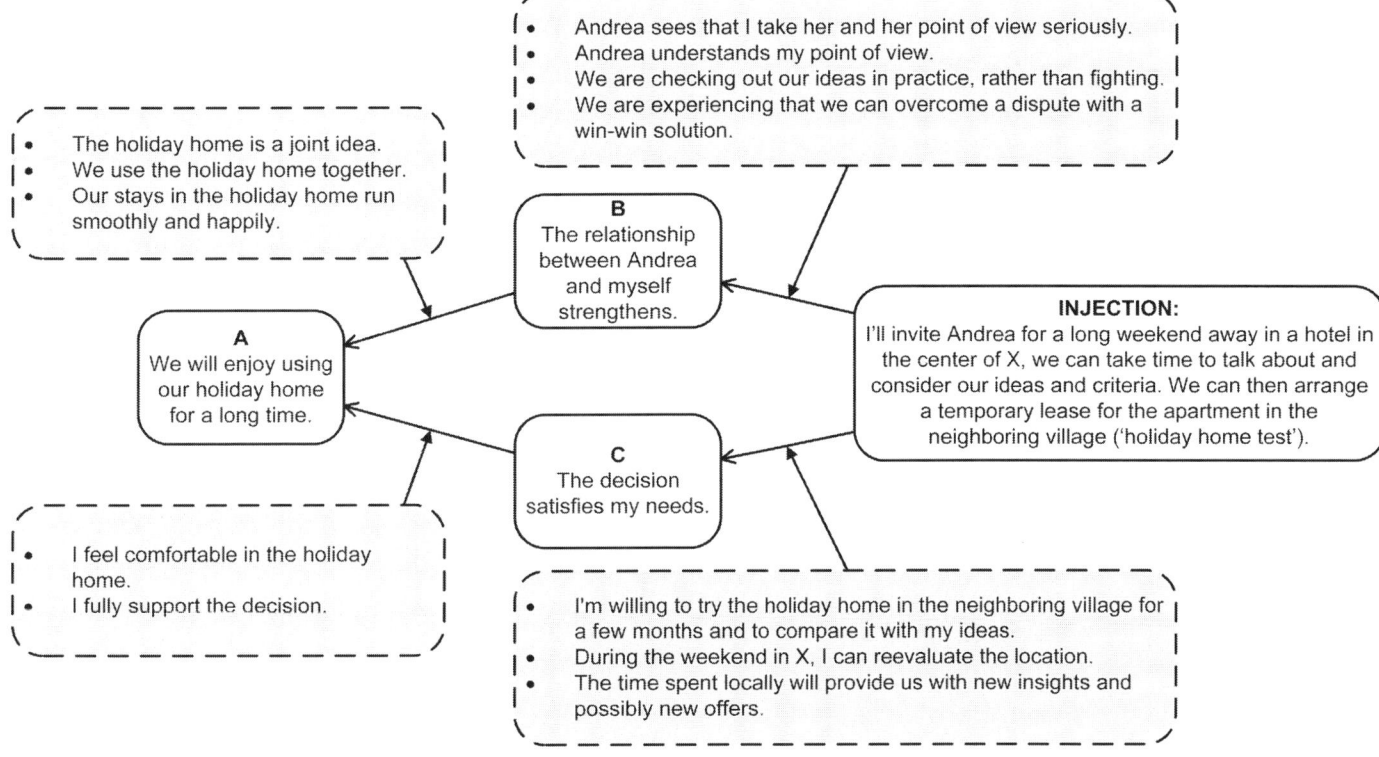

Workbook Win-Win Solutions

4.6.3 My solution—1. outline

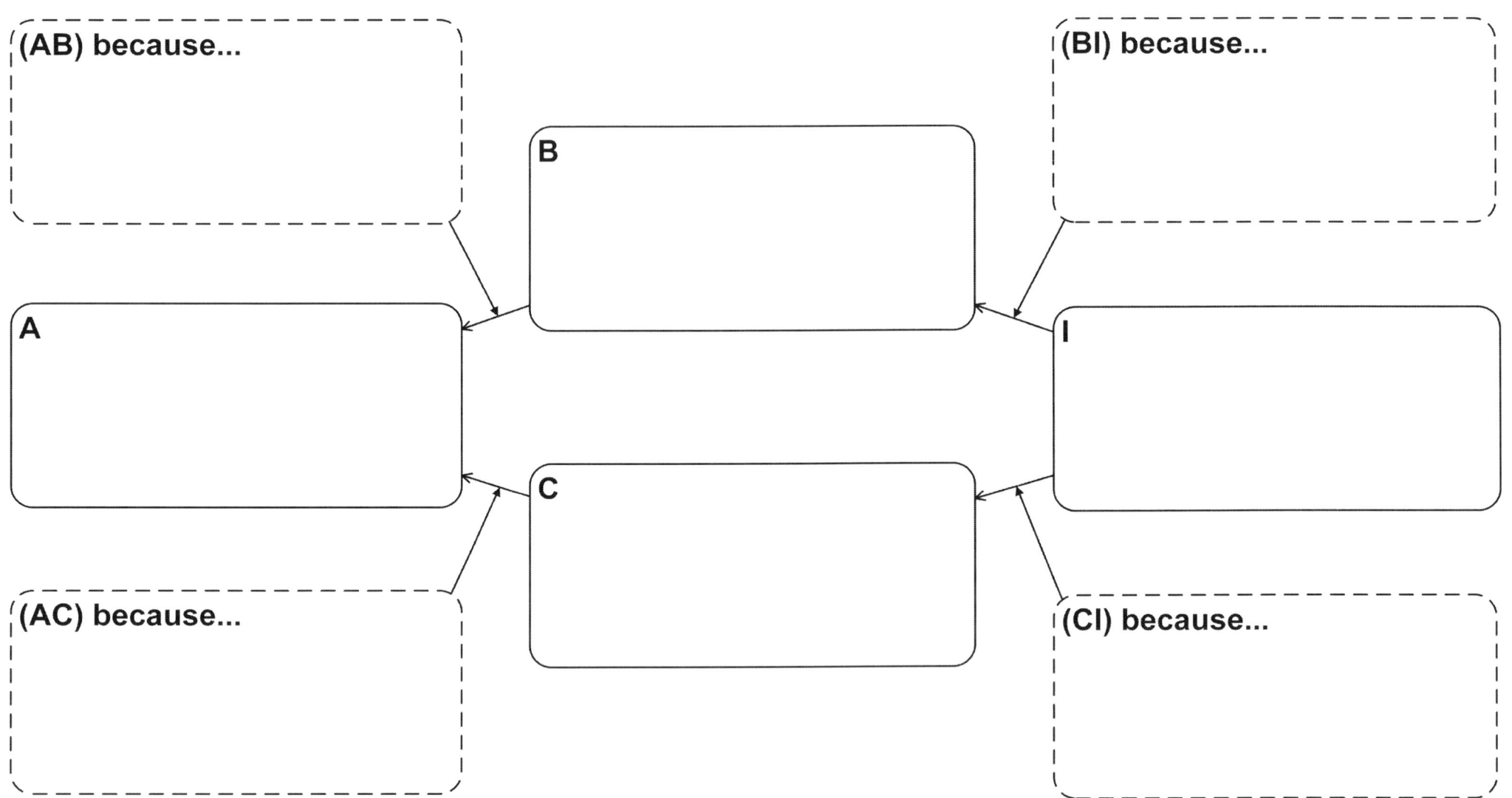

4.6.4 My solution—2. outline

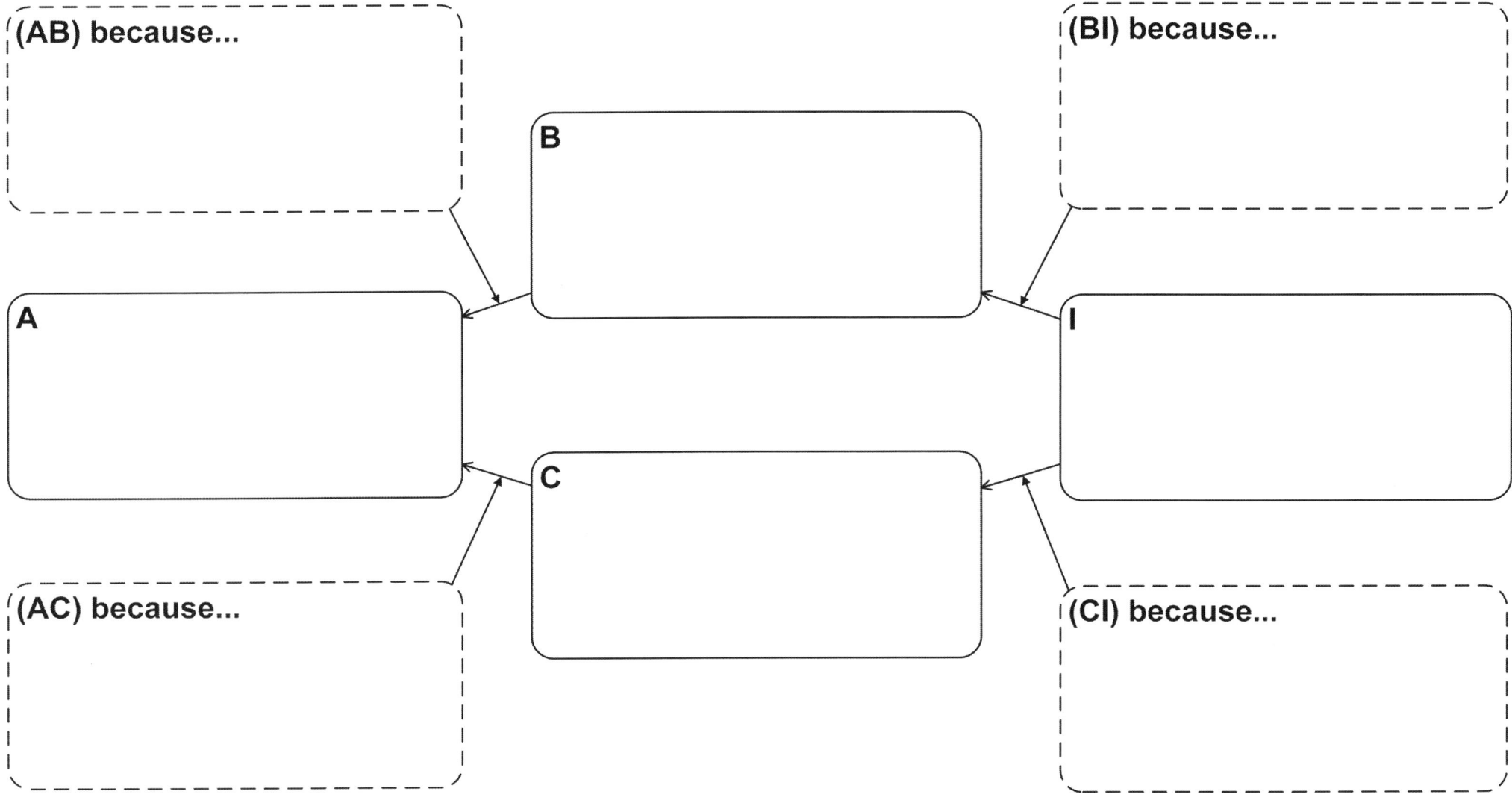

Dilemma

5 Dilemma — exercise 3

5.1 Problem report

Title / topic
Report

5.2. Possible actions

Action	Pressure from system / others	I would like to...

Pressure	
Preferred	

5.3 Dilemma

5.3.1 Dilemma — 1. outline

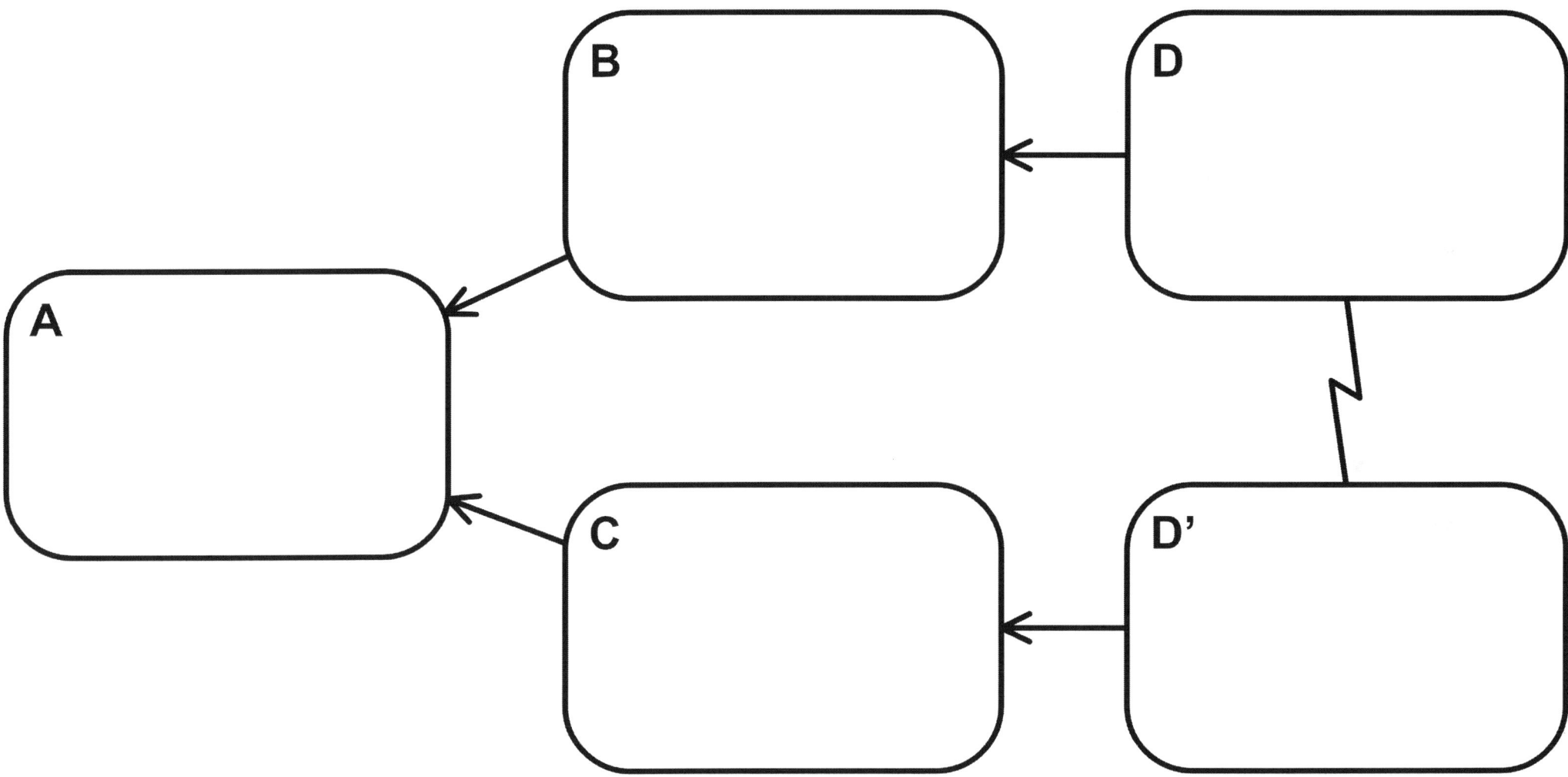

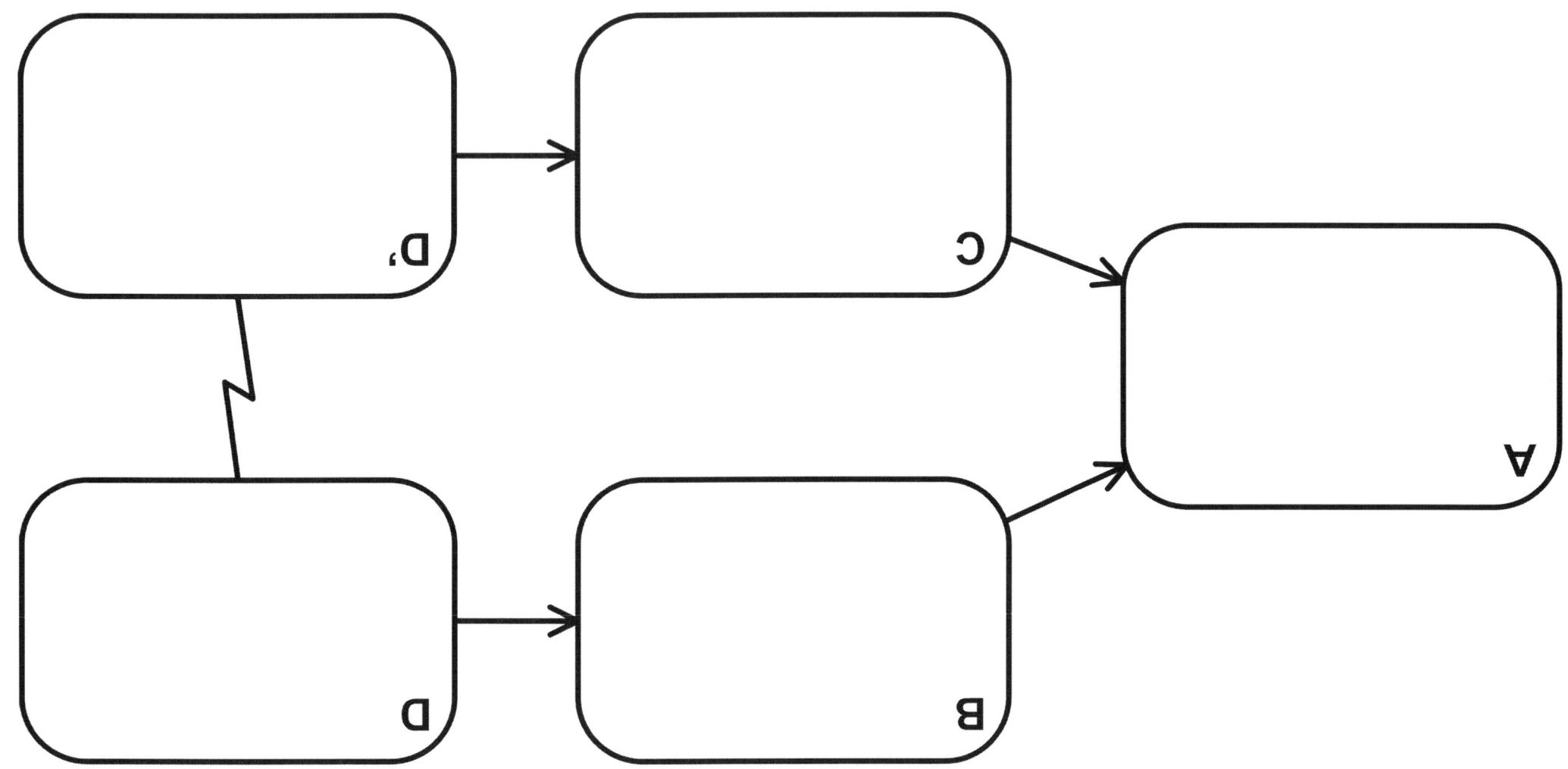

5.3.2 Dilemma-2. outline

5.3.3 Dilemma with assumptions — 1. outline

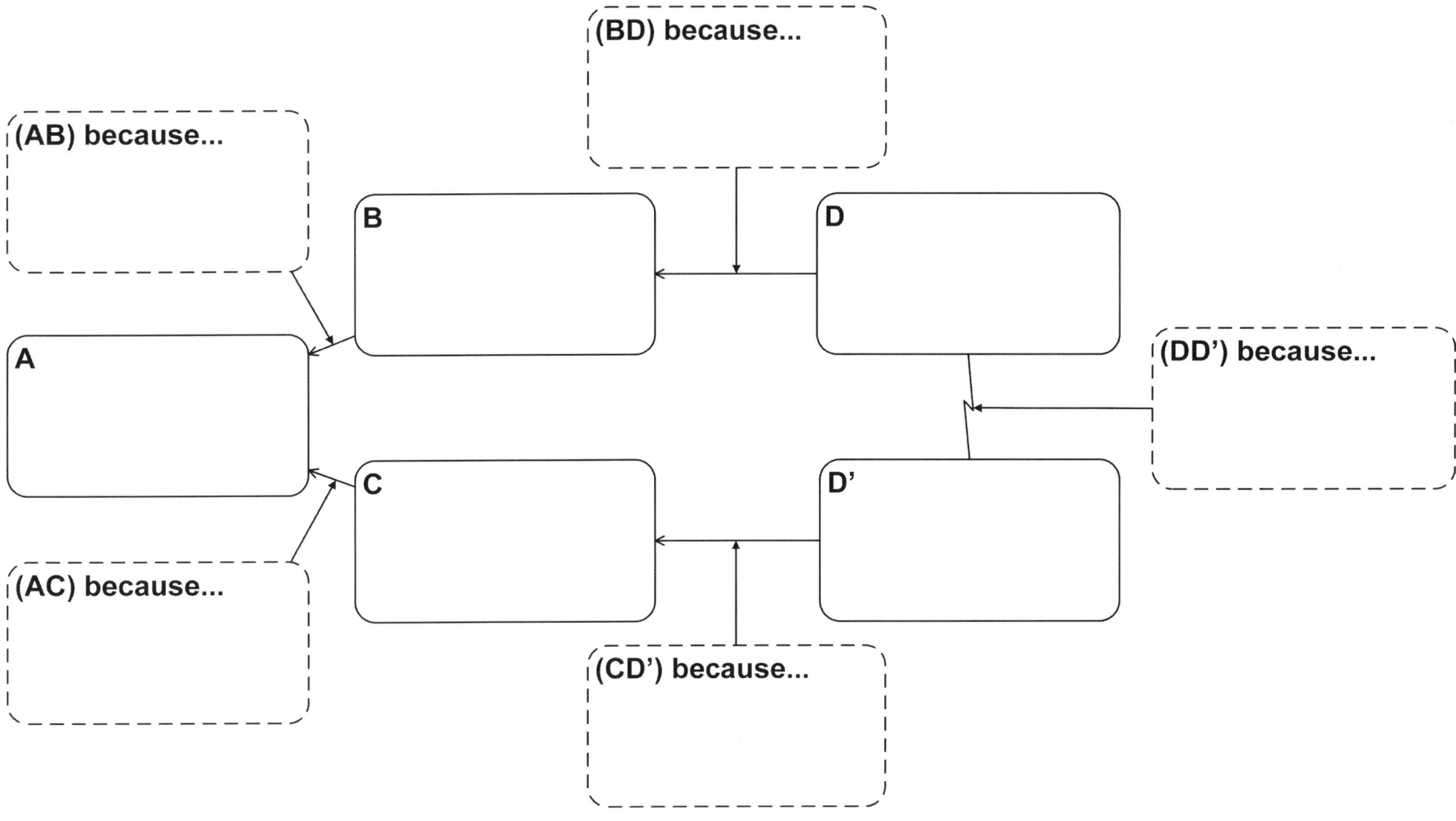

Workbook Win-Win Solutions 52

5.3.4   Dilemma with assumptions — 2. outline

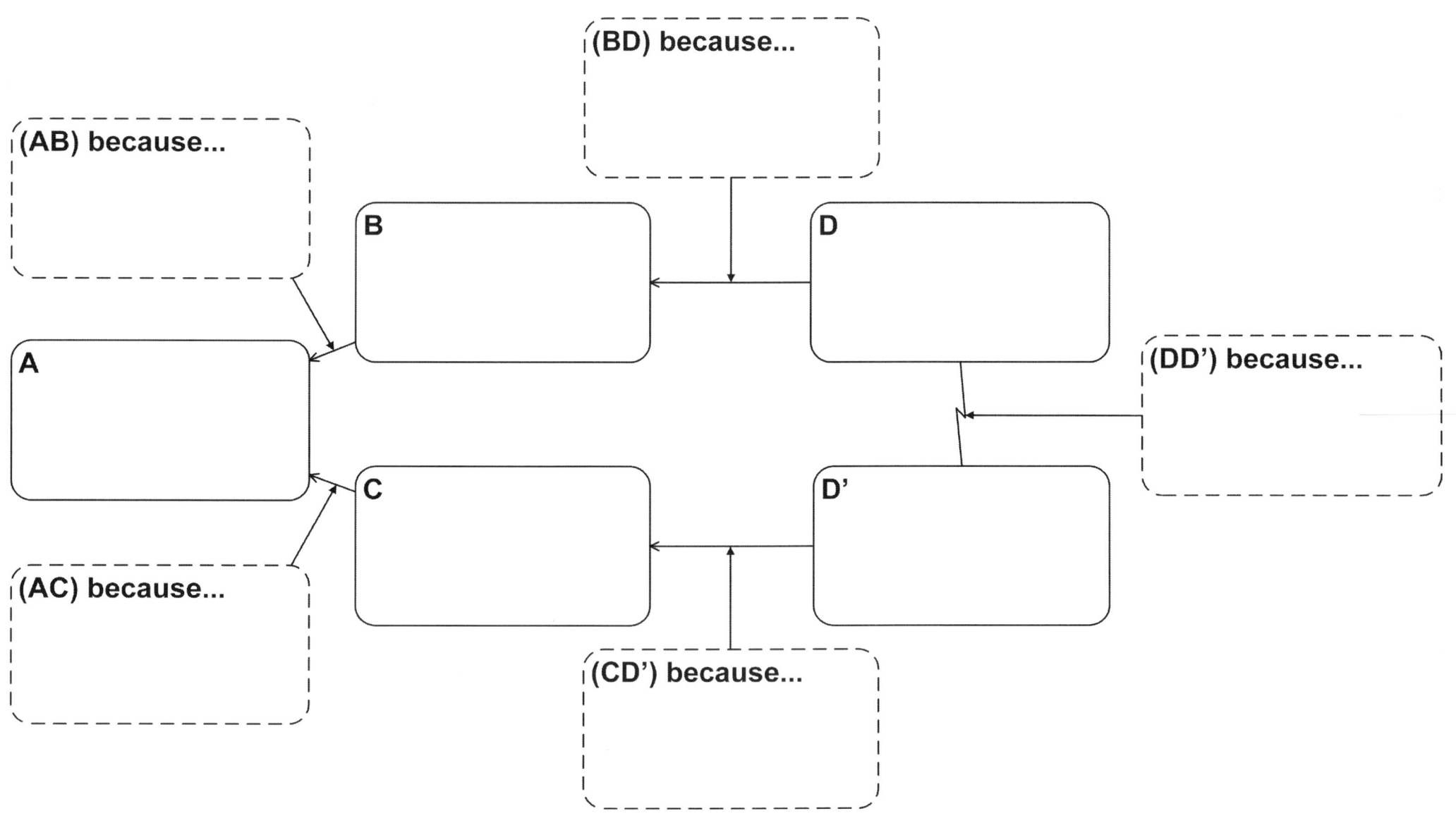

5.4 Possible solutions

	Reasons / assumptions	Possible solutions
A-B		
A-C		
B-D		
C-D′		
D-D′		

5.5 Solution

5.5.1 Solution — 1. outline

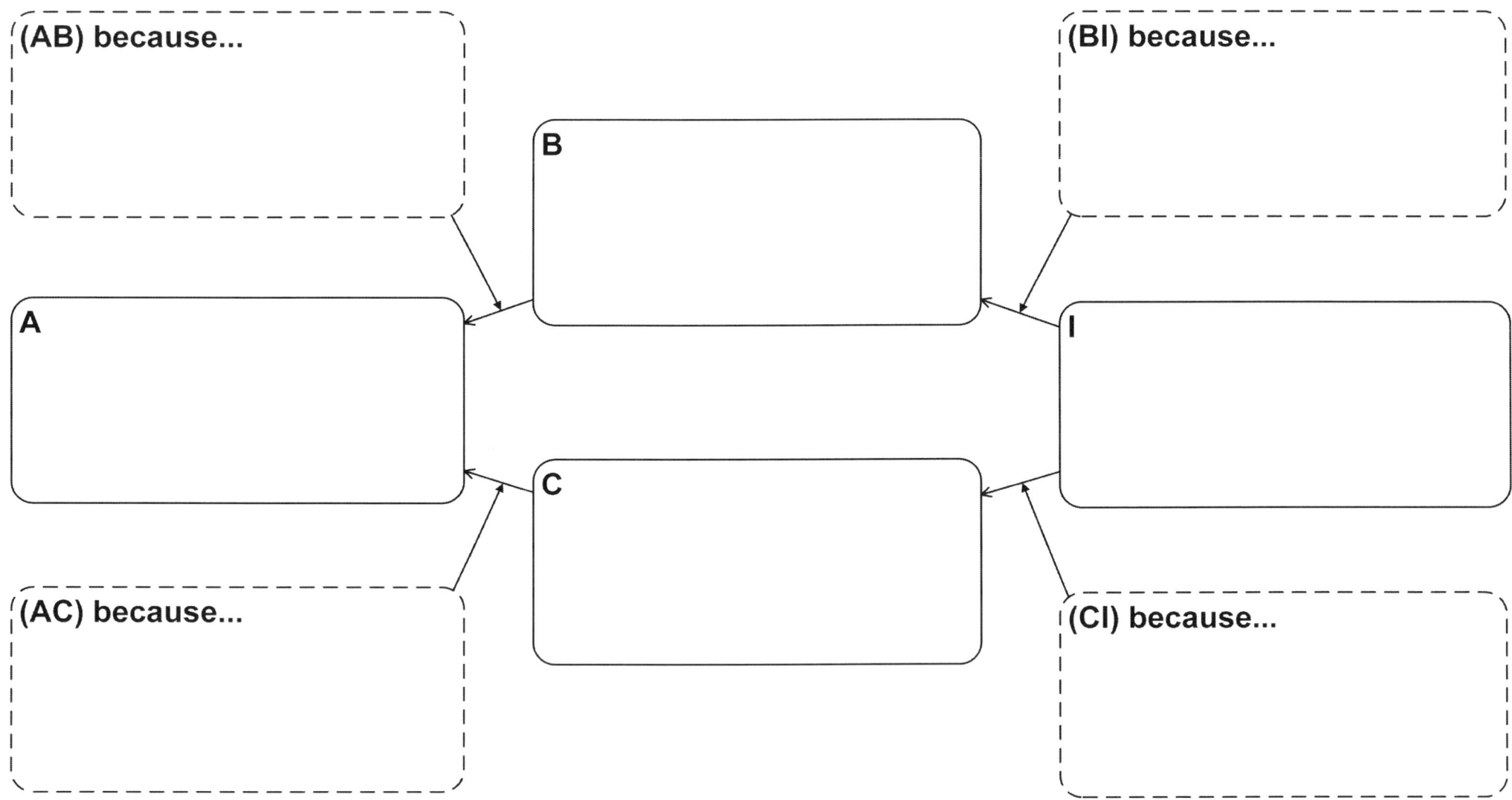

5.5.2 Solution — 2. outline

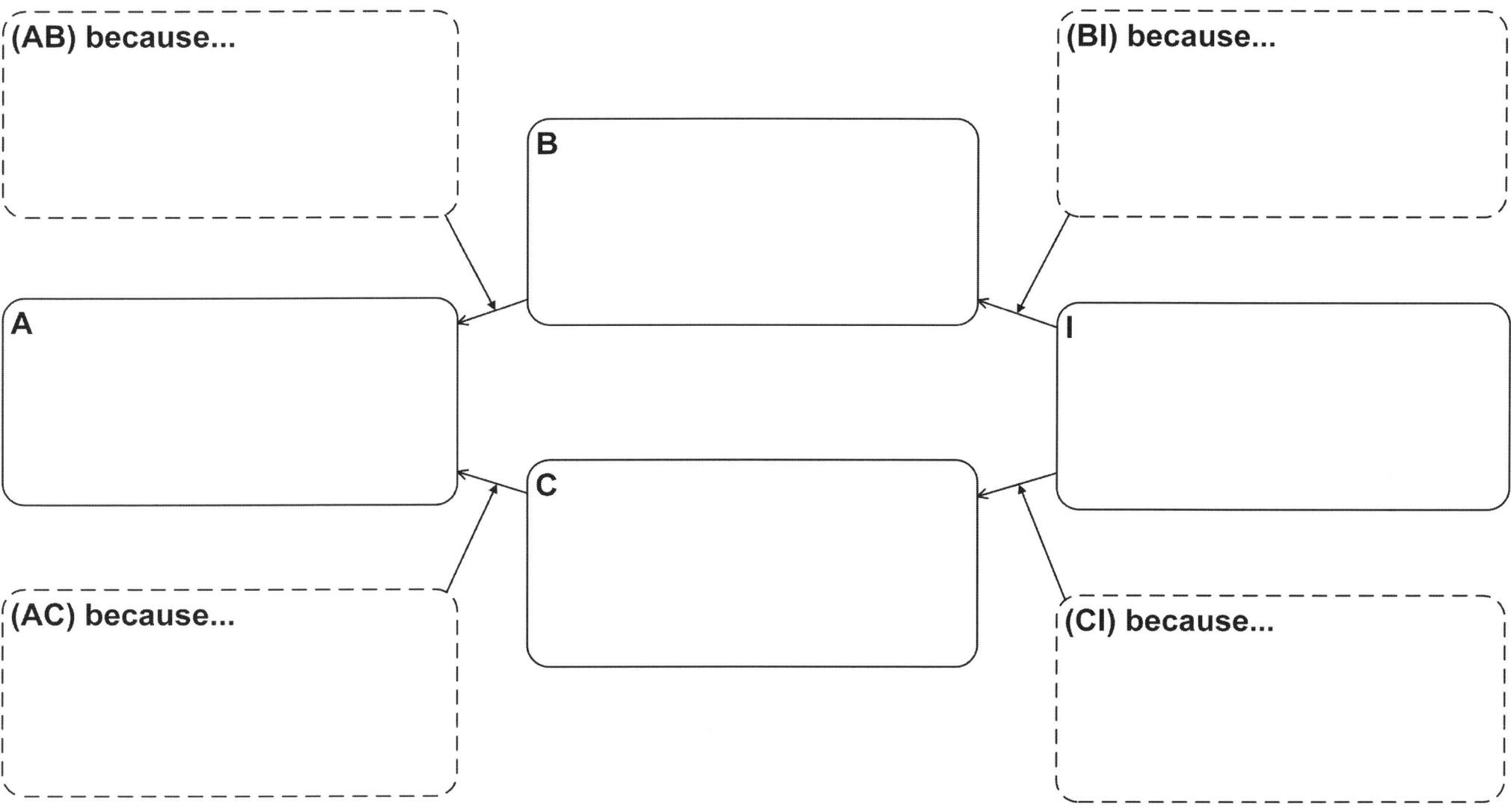

Dilemma

6 Dilemma — exercise 4

6.1 Problem report

Title / topic
Report

6.2   Possible actions

Action	Pressure from system / others	I would like to...

Pressure	
Preferred	

6.3 Dilemma

6.3.1 Dilemma — 1. outline

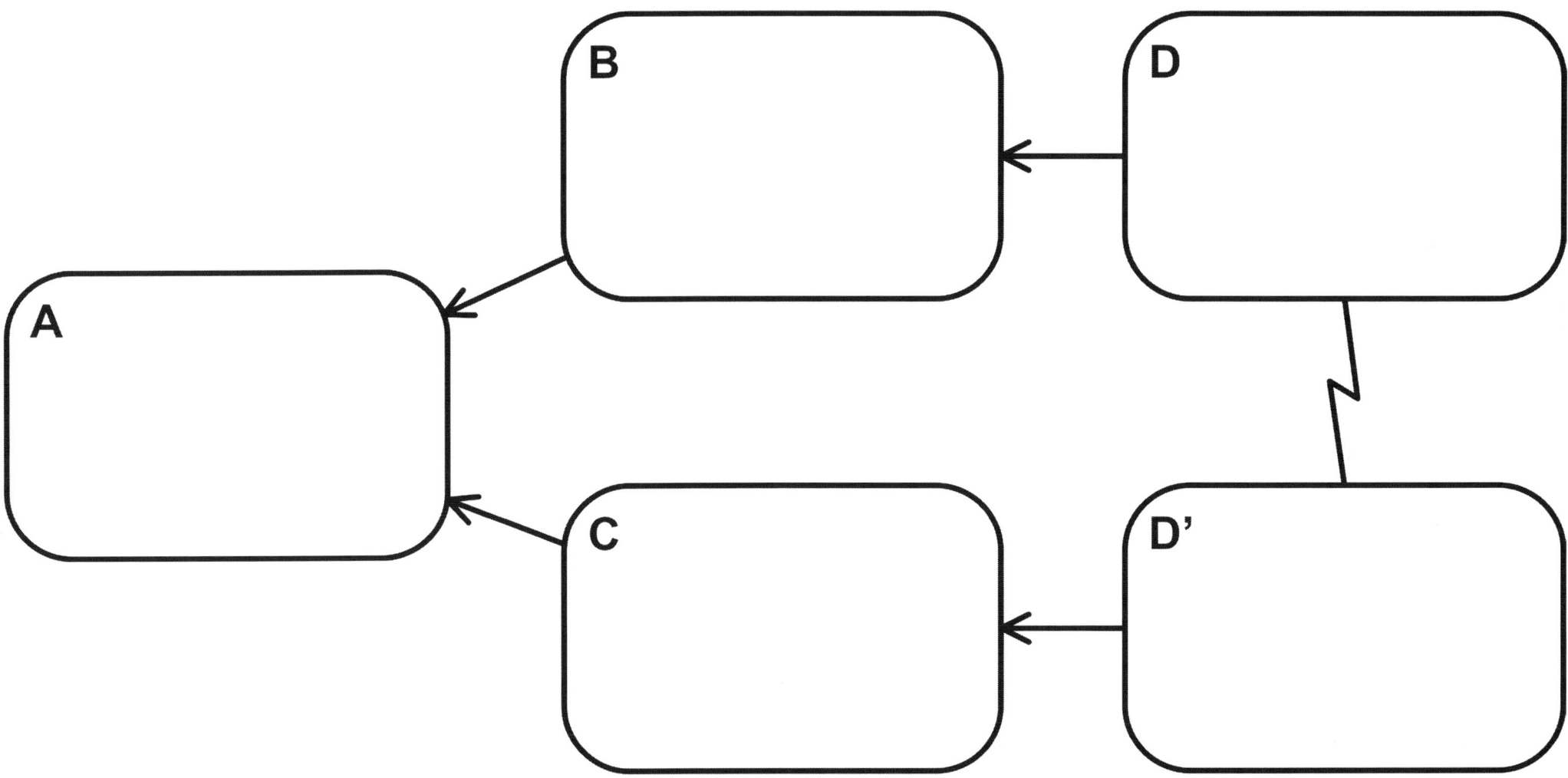

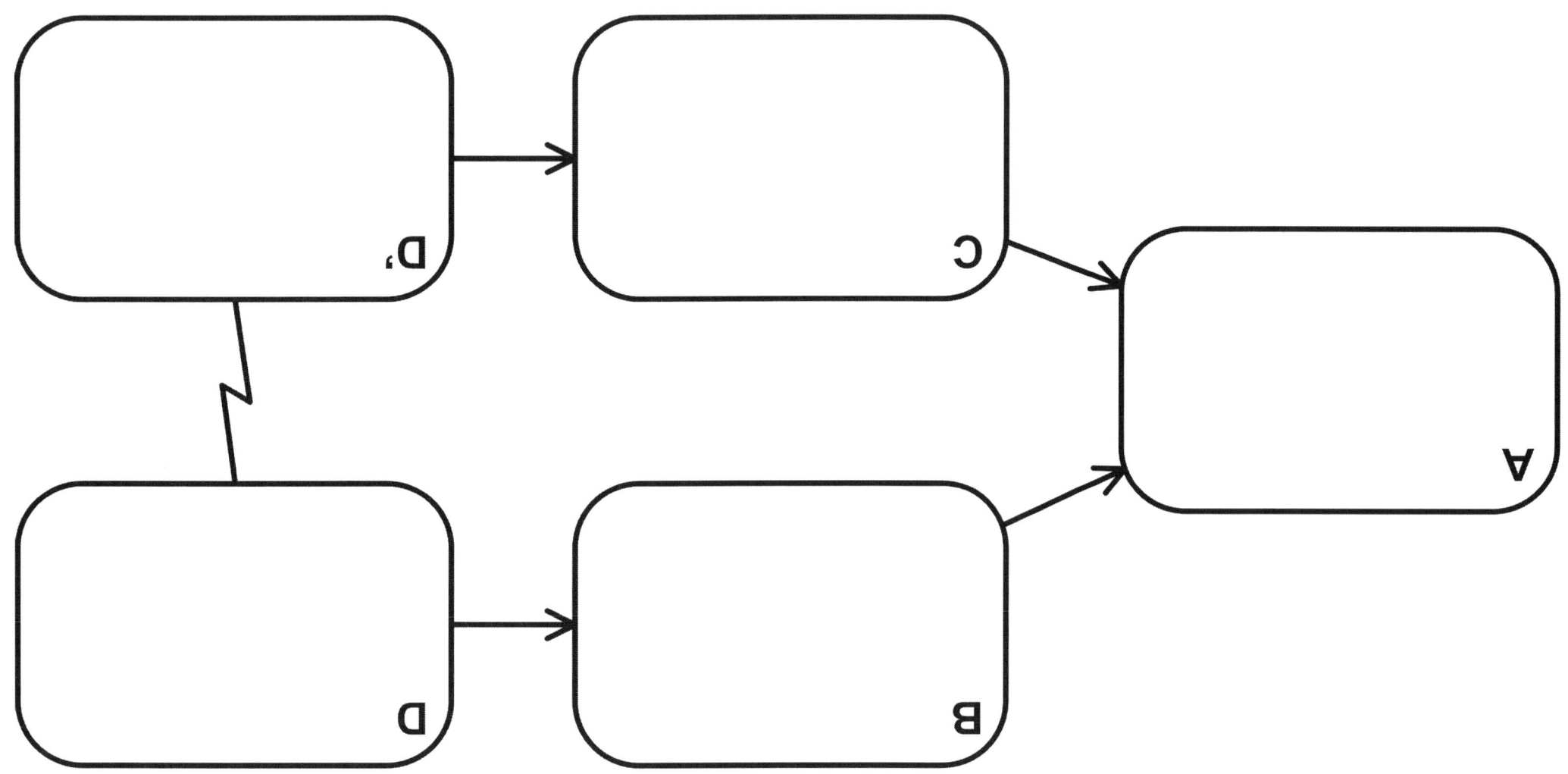

6.3.2 Dilemma-2. outline

6.3.3 Dilemma with assumptions — 1. outline

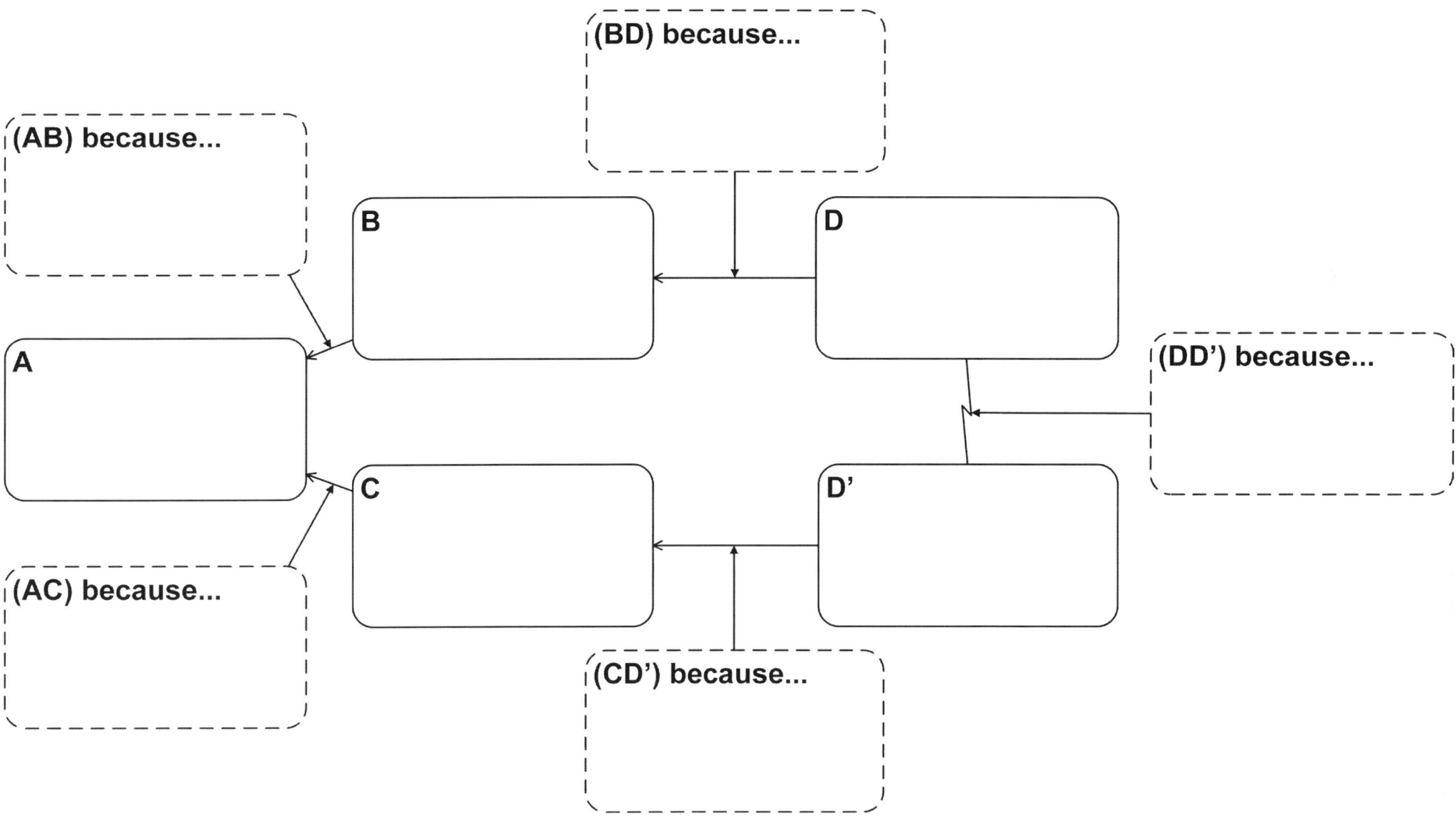

Workbook Win-Win Solutions

6.3.4 Dilemma with assumptions — 2. outline

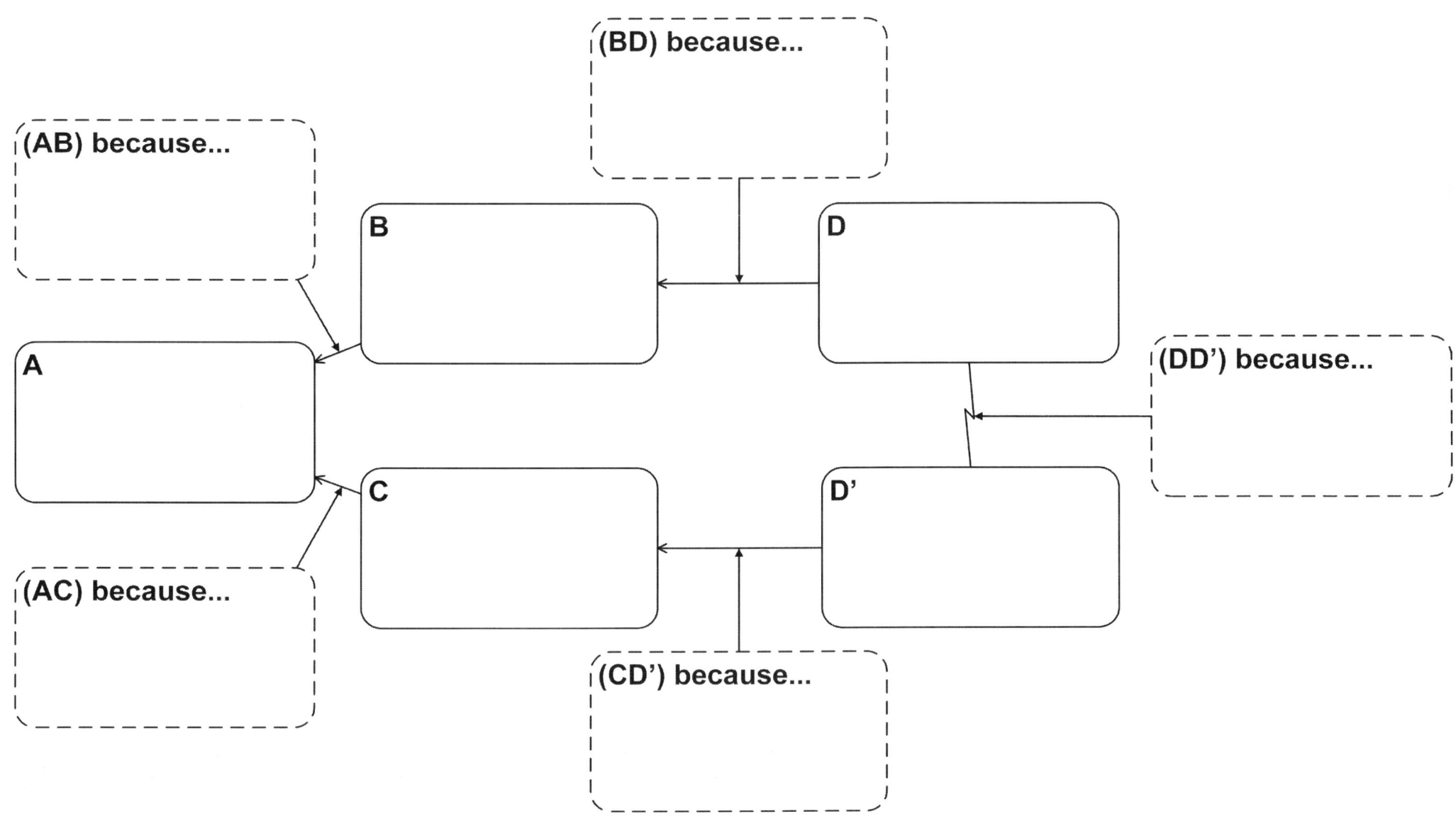

6.4 Possible solutions

	Reasons / assumptions	Possible solutions
A-B		
A-C		
B-D		
C-D'		
D-D'		

Workbook Win-Win Solutions

6.5 Solution

6.5.1 Solution — 1. outline

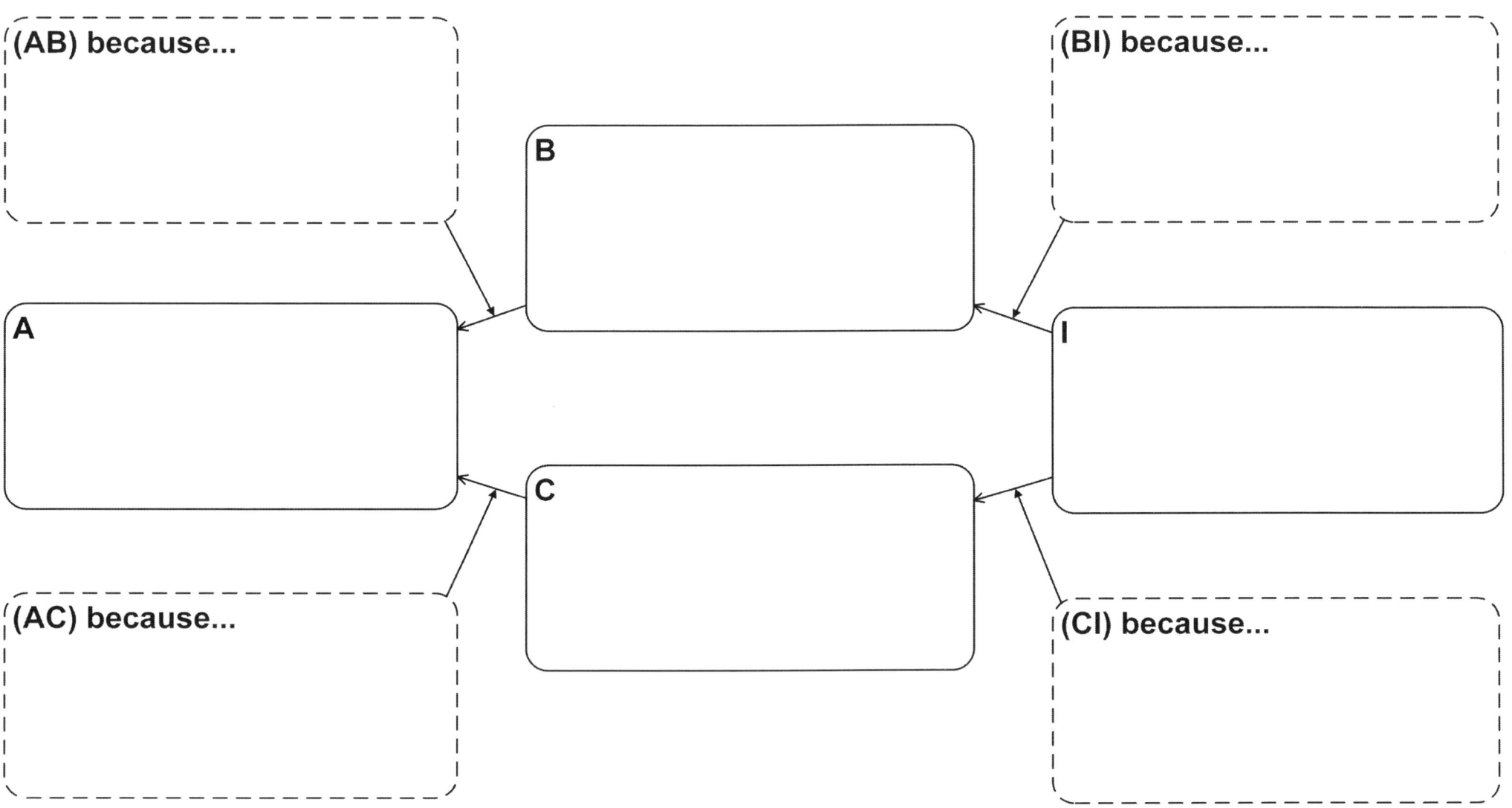

6.5.2 Solution—2. outline

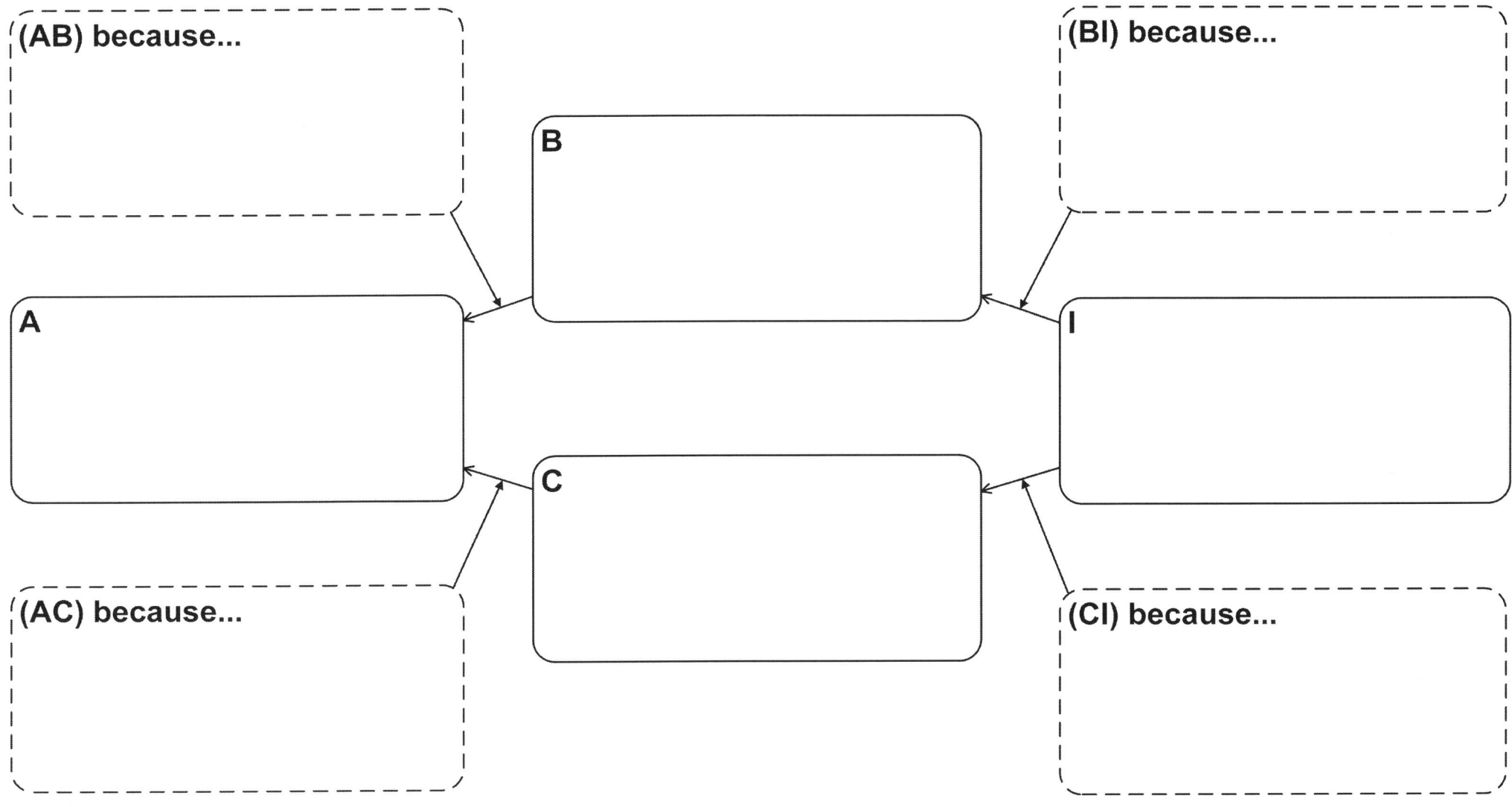

Dilemma

7 Dilemma — exercise 5

7.1 Problem report

Title / topic
Report

Workbook Win-Win Solutions 68

7.2. Possible actions

Action	Pressure from system / others	I would like to...

Pressure	
Preferred	

7.3 Dilemma

7.3.1 Dilemma — 1. outline

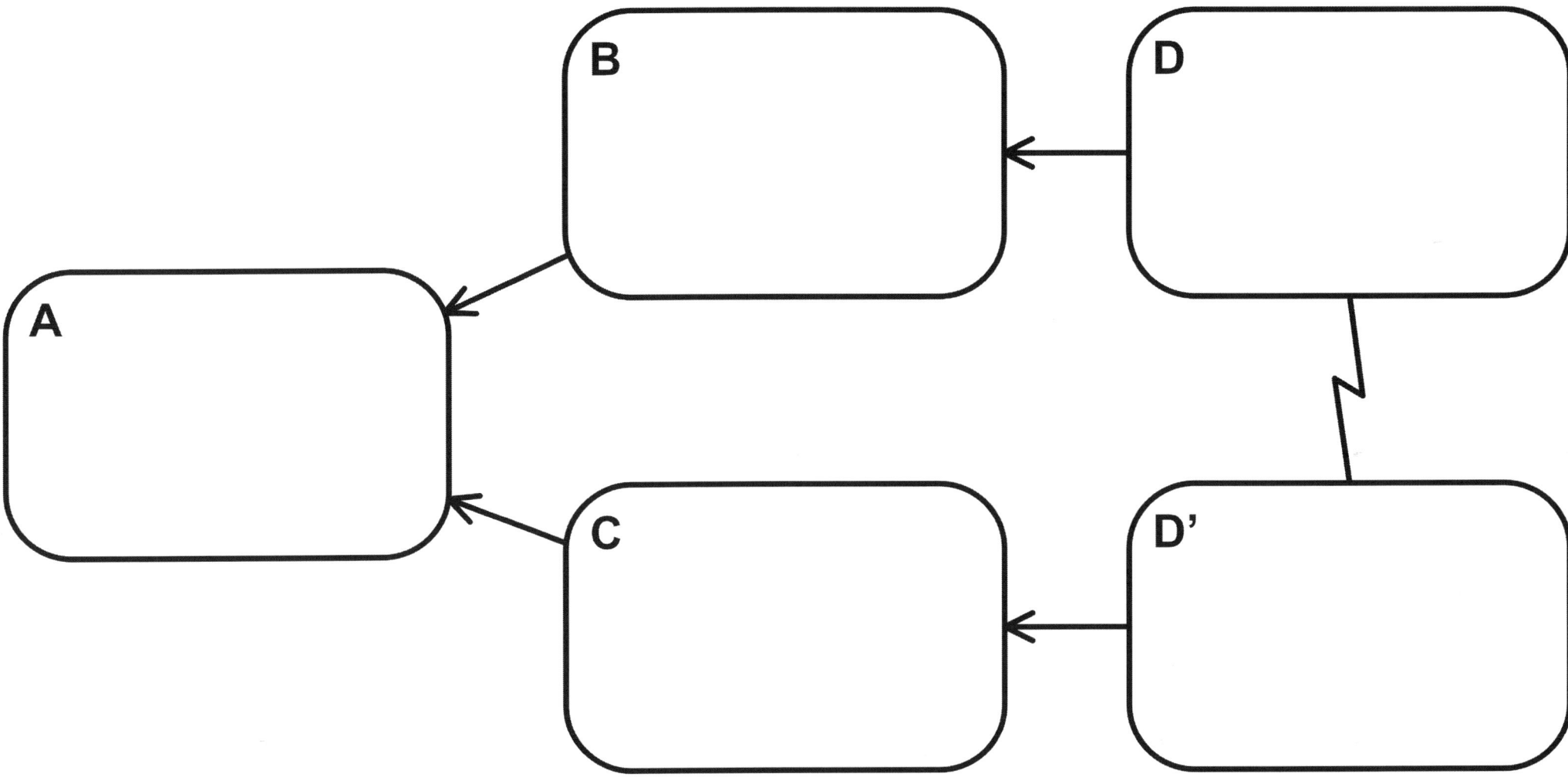

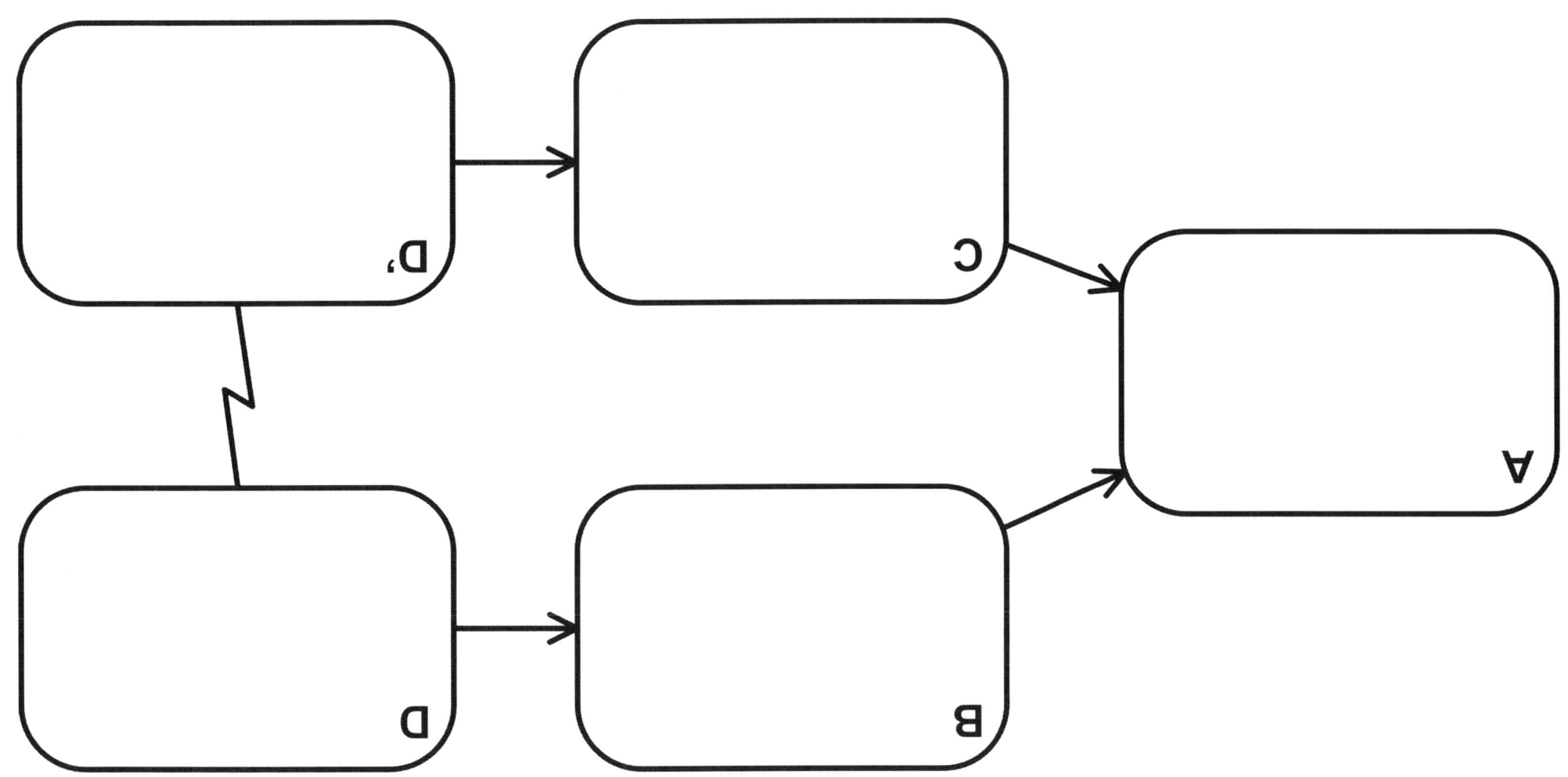

7.3.3 Dilemma with assumptions — 1. outline

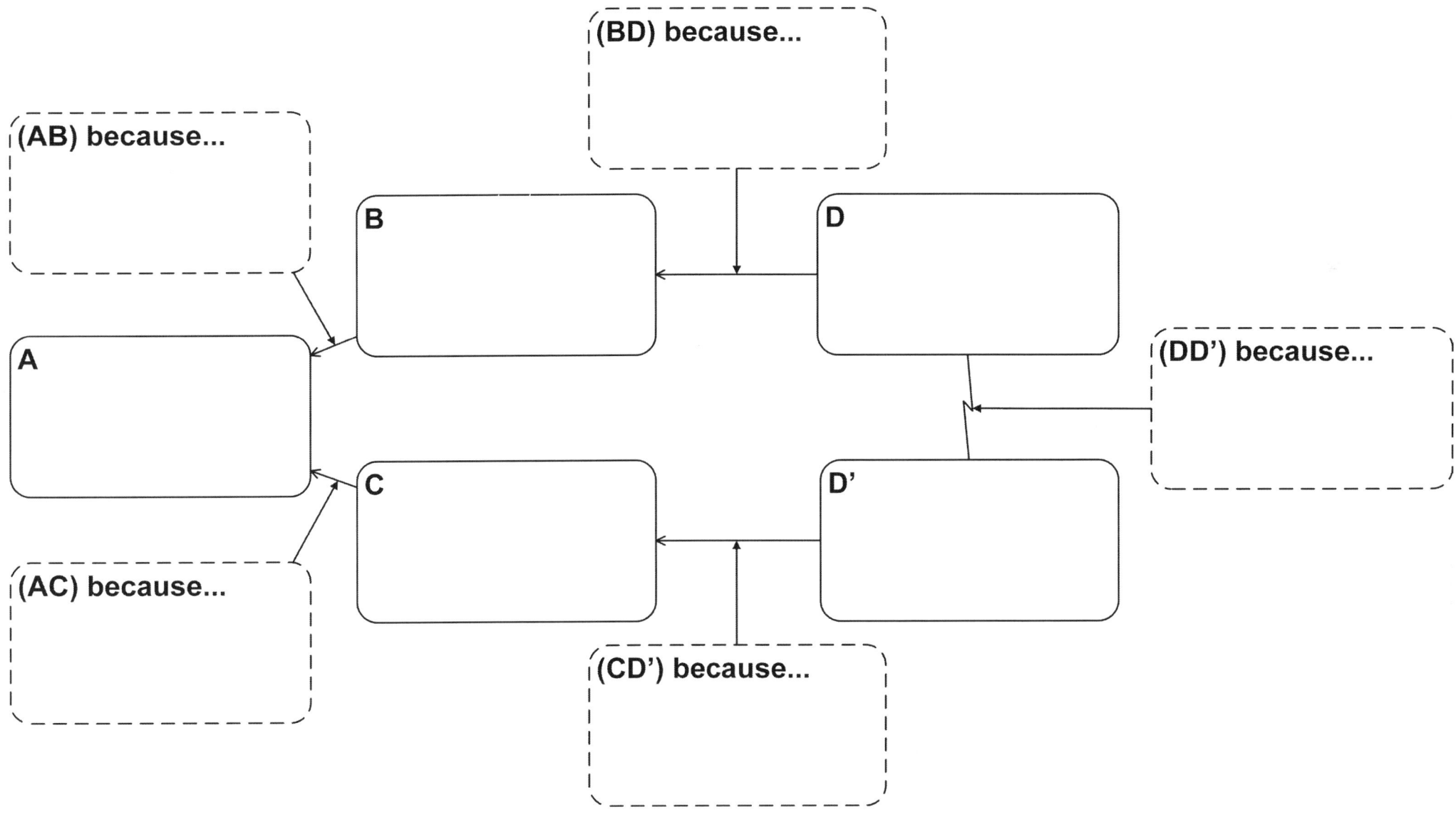

Workbook Win-Win Solutions

7.3.4 Dilemma with assumptions—2. outline

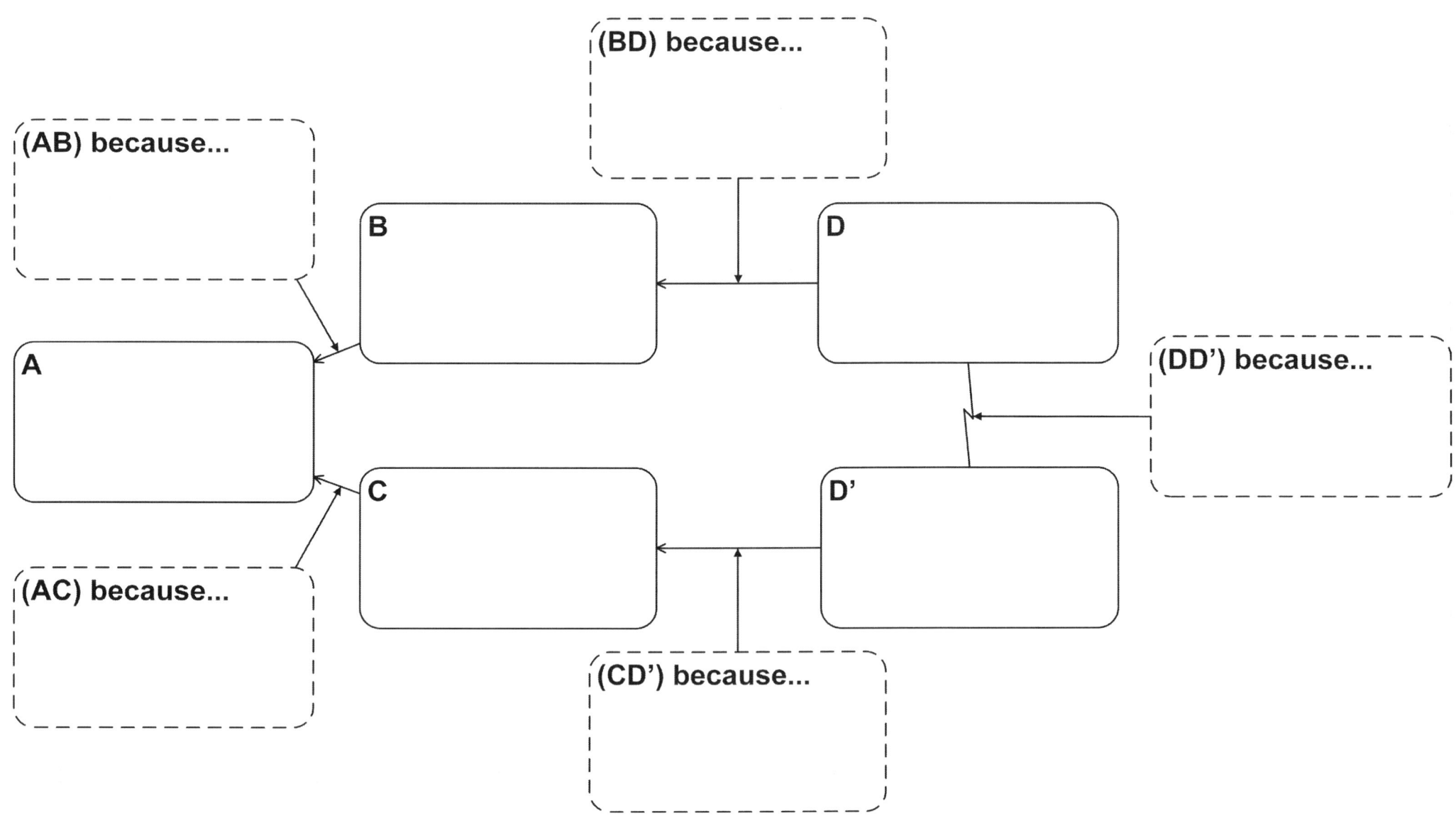

7.4 Possible solutions

	Reasons / assumptions	Possible solutions
A-B		
A-C		
B-D		
C-D'		
D-D'		

7.5 Solution

7.5.1 Solution — 1. outline

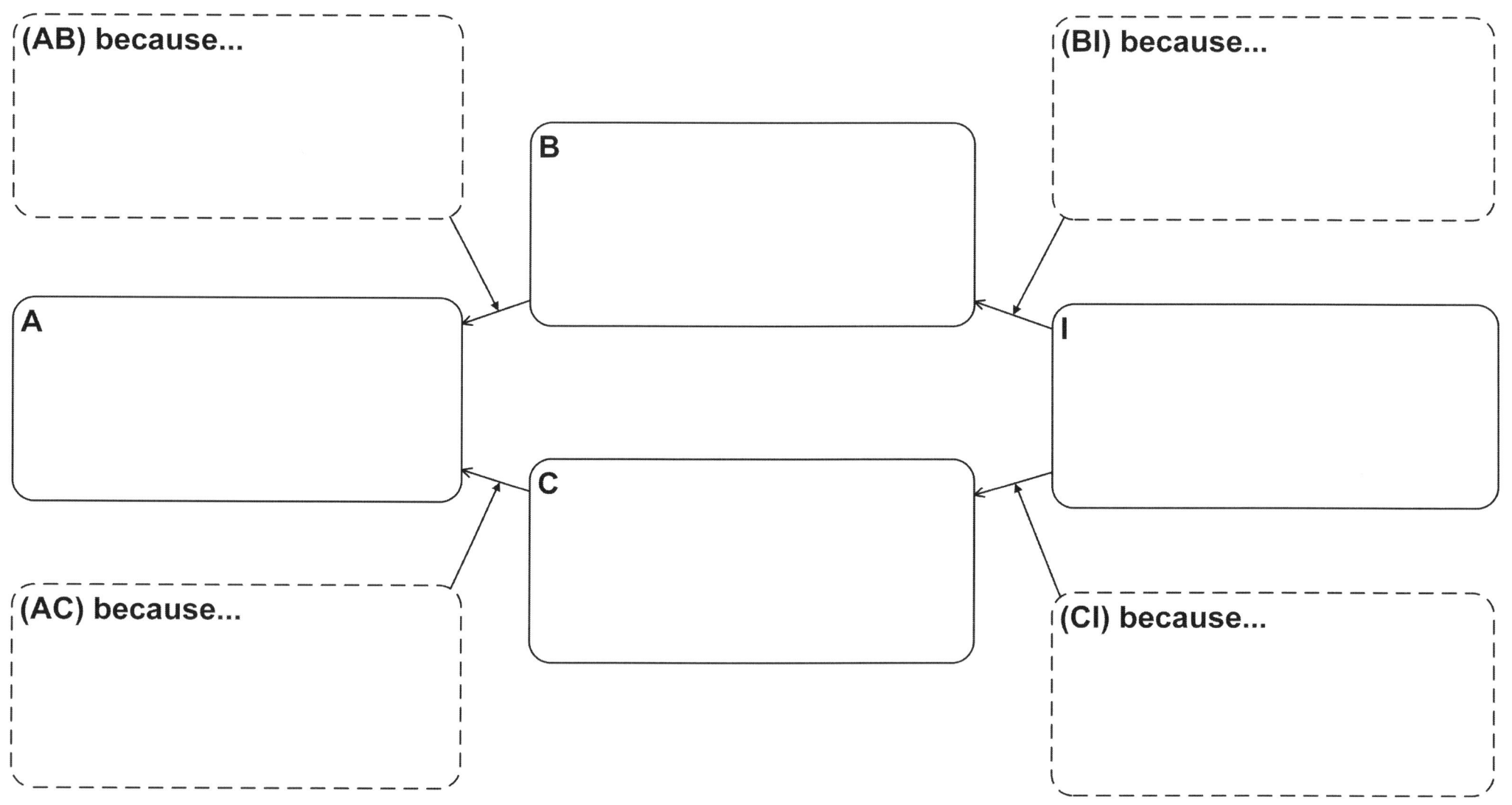

7.5.2 Solution — 2. outline

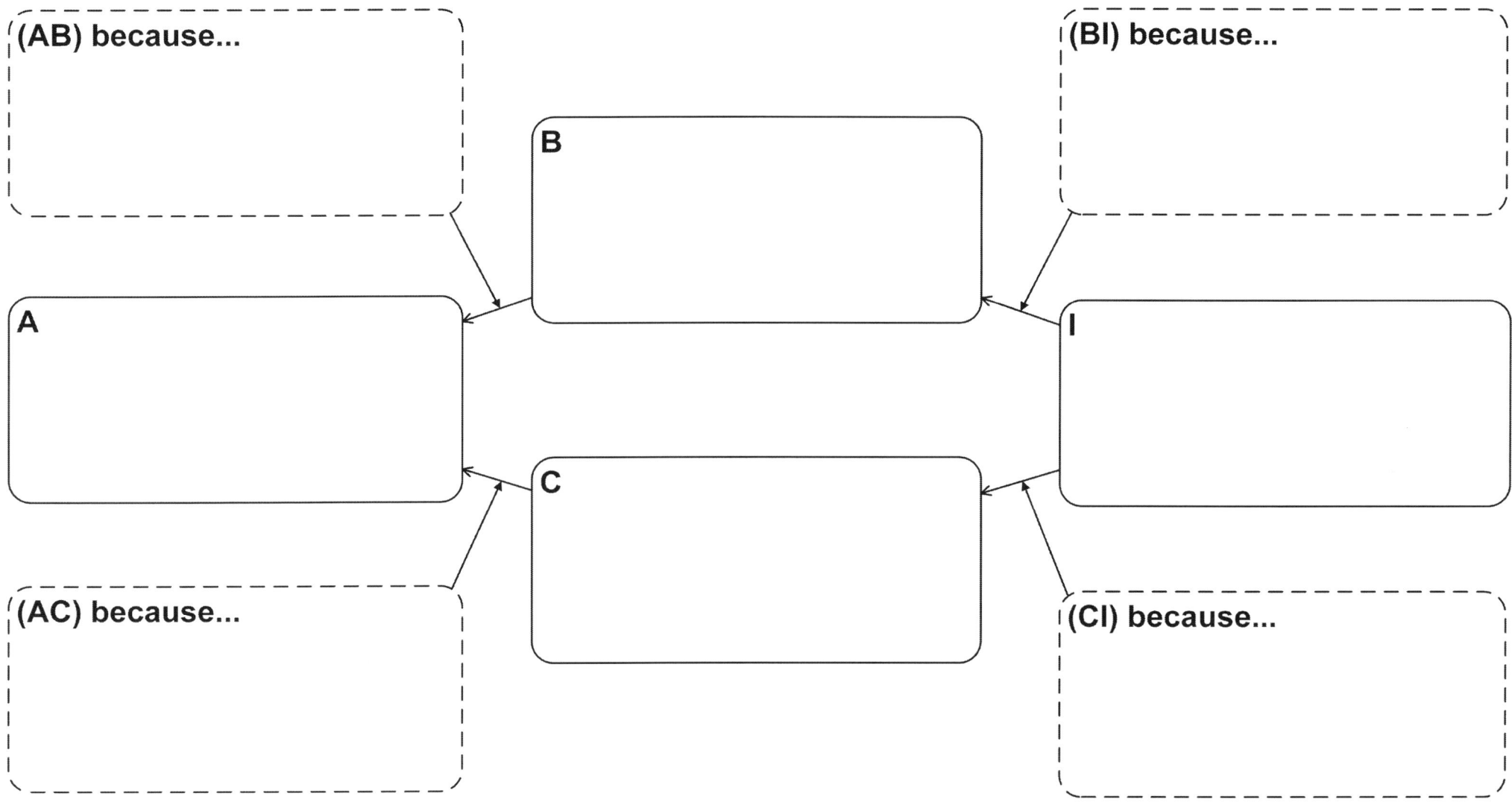

8 Dilemma — summary and instructions for completion

1. Describe the situation.
2. Determine the action alternatives, why do you feel pressured, what do you actually prefer to do?
3. Fill in the Cloud Diagram and check the logic, adjust the formulations and carry out a cross match. Formulate your assumptions.
4. Question the assumptions and seek possible solutions.
5. Represent the solution in the diagram, check your logic, in particular, whether the needs and objective can be achieved: Justify these relationships with appropriate assumptions.

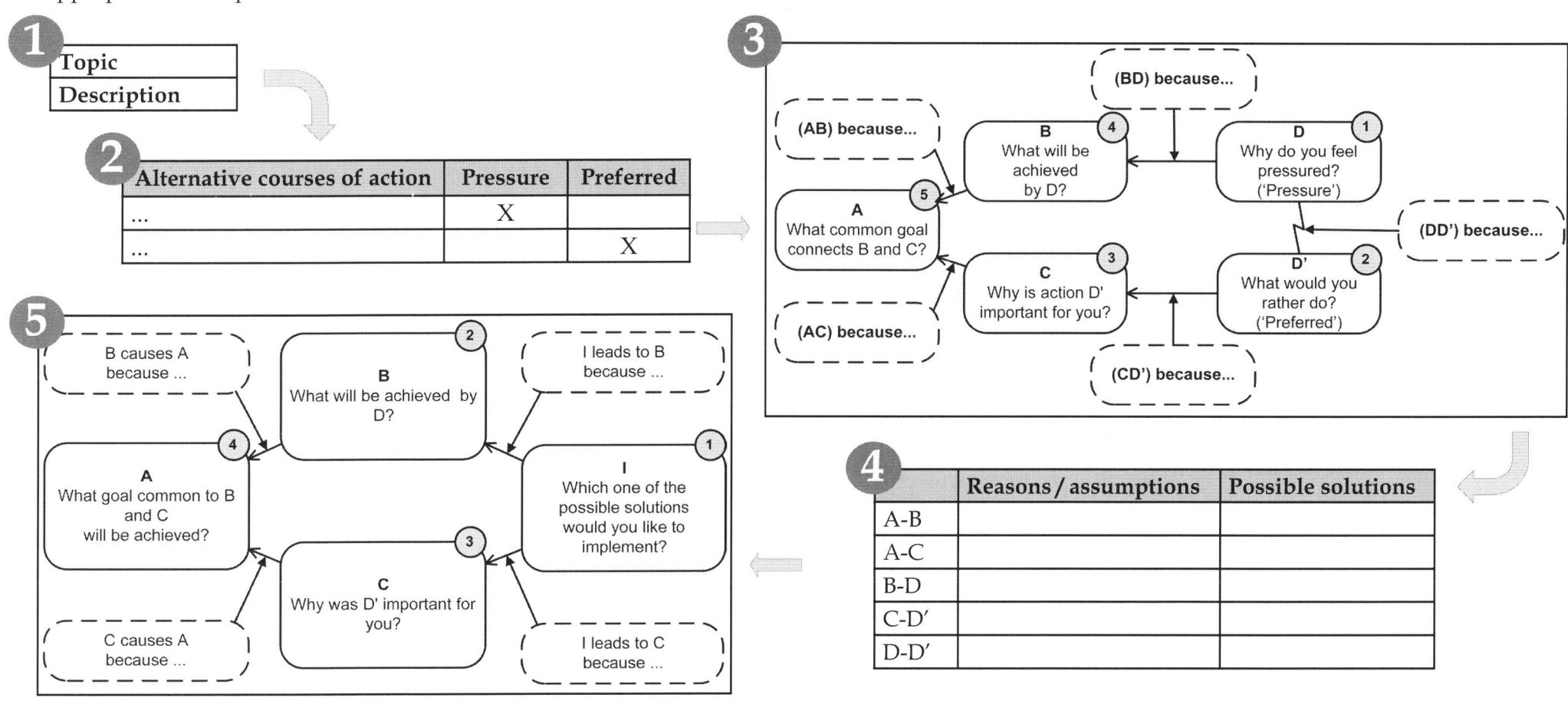

9 Fire (inconsistency between tasks and competences)

A 'fire' describes a situation in which there is inconsistency between the tasks a person needs to perform and the requisite skills, or in other words, between responsibility and scope for decision making.

A fire occurs whenever an employee approaches you (we assume you are their superior) and finds themselves in one of the following situations:

- Due to their role or function within the company—in order to carry out their work properly—they need to carry out a certain action.
- Due to their role or function they may not be able to specifically carry out this action, because they would be contravening an existing rule in the company.

Caught in this predicament, the person comes to you with their dilemma and expects guidelines on how they should act.

A 'fire' is created,

- when there is a difference between tasks and responsibility on the one hand, and the skills an employee has on the other; or:
- If there are rules in the company, which are contradictory.

The employee finds themselves in a conflict situation: whatever they do, is wrong. Or in other words: if they do the 'right' thing, then they will be contravening the rules. Therefore, they ask you, their superior, to put out the fire.

9.1 Recently encountered fire

9.1.1 Instructions

1. Create a list of five recently encountered situations that were annoying, because they 'really' did not require your participation (others were responsible or in charge).

2. Bear in mind that the situations need to meet the following conditions:
   - You had to put out a fire or solve a problem for an employee.
   - It was a topic with which you wanted to have nothing to do.

3. Perhaps, you were under a certain amount of pressure to take action and resolve the matter.

4. Summarize each situation in one sentence.

9.1.2 Examples

- There was an incident regarding a delivery to a specific customer and the shipping address.
- My Assistant had to fetch me out of a meeting to get a decision on booking a courier.
- Our new image brochures could be not delivered on time by the printer. I had to decide whether we should accept a part-delivery and then delivery of the remainder within 5 days.
- One of our customers had gone over their credit limit and I had to call the credit insurer from my holiday to ask as guarantor.

9.2 Fire list (recently encountered fire)

1.	
2.	
3.	
4.	
5.	
6.	
7.	
8.	
9.	

10 Fire — exercise 1 (with full instructions)

10.1 Fire report

10.1.1 Instructions

1. Write a report on your 'fire' — as if you were writing an essay or a letter of complaint.

2. Take into account the following questions:
   - Who came to you and with what concerns?
   - Why does that person have to come to you?
   - What concrete decision did you have to make?

The purpose of the Report is to help you put the facts and your thoughts on the selected problem down on paper, so they can be subsequently processed and structured.

10.1.2 Example

Title / topic	There was an incident regarding a delivery to a specific customer and the shipping address.
Report	I am a customer service manager at XYZ Co. Yesterday, one of my employees, the Dispatch Manager, came to me and asked for help. It was related to a delivery for a customer. Yesterday was the last possible delivery date, but the shipping address was unclear. The key-account manager for that customer, who is also subordinate to me, has been unavailable for the last three days due to an overseas business trip. So I had to call the customer. It took several attempts and clarifications. Finally, I obtained the delivery address, passed it on to the dispatch manager and continued with my other work.

10.2 My fire report

Title / topic	
Report	

10.3 Fire Cloud

10.3.1 Instructions

Create Fire Clouds in the following order:

1. C: The need of the system that is at risk. Why does the employee need to act?

2. D: The rule, which prevents the employe from meeting the need of C. What is stopping them from acting?

3. D': Action that is required to meet the need. What will they do?

4. The need of the system that is fulfilled by rule D. Why is the action prohibited?

5. A: The smallest common goal of B and C. What connects the reason for the prohibition (B) and the employee's motivation (C)?

6. Read through the Fire Cloud, and check the formulations and the logic:
   - (To achieve) A, I need to (ensure) B.
   - (To achieve) A, I need to (ensure) C.
   - (To achieve) B, D needs (to be maintained).
   - (To achieve) C, D' has (to be done).

7. Additional review:
   - Does D' endanger the existence of B?
   - Does D endanger the existence of C?
   - Does D' endanger the existence of A?
   - Are D and D' clear opposites or exclusive courses of action?

10.3.2 Example

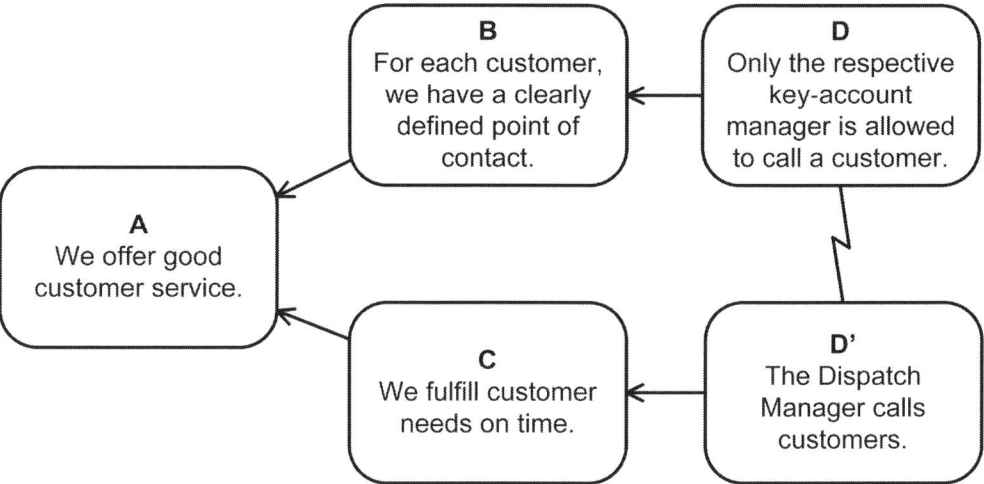

10.3.3 Next steps

- Make the required decision immediately.
- Then construct a Fire Cloud for yourself (alone) [sequence: C, D, D', B, A].
- Introduce the Fire Cloud to the employee [sequence: A, C, D', D, B].
- Together with the employee, identify the assumptions.
- Together with the employee, resolve the connection between B and D.
- Represent the Win-Win Solution graphically.

Workbook Win-Win Solutions

10.4 My Fire Cloud

10.4.1 Fire Cloud—1. outline

Note: You will probably end up revising your formulations several times. Therefore, it might be a good idea to use sticky notes initially, instead of writing directly on the paper. Alternatively, you can revise your formulations on the following pages.

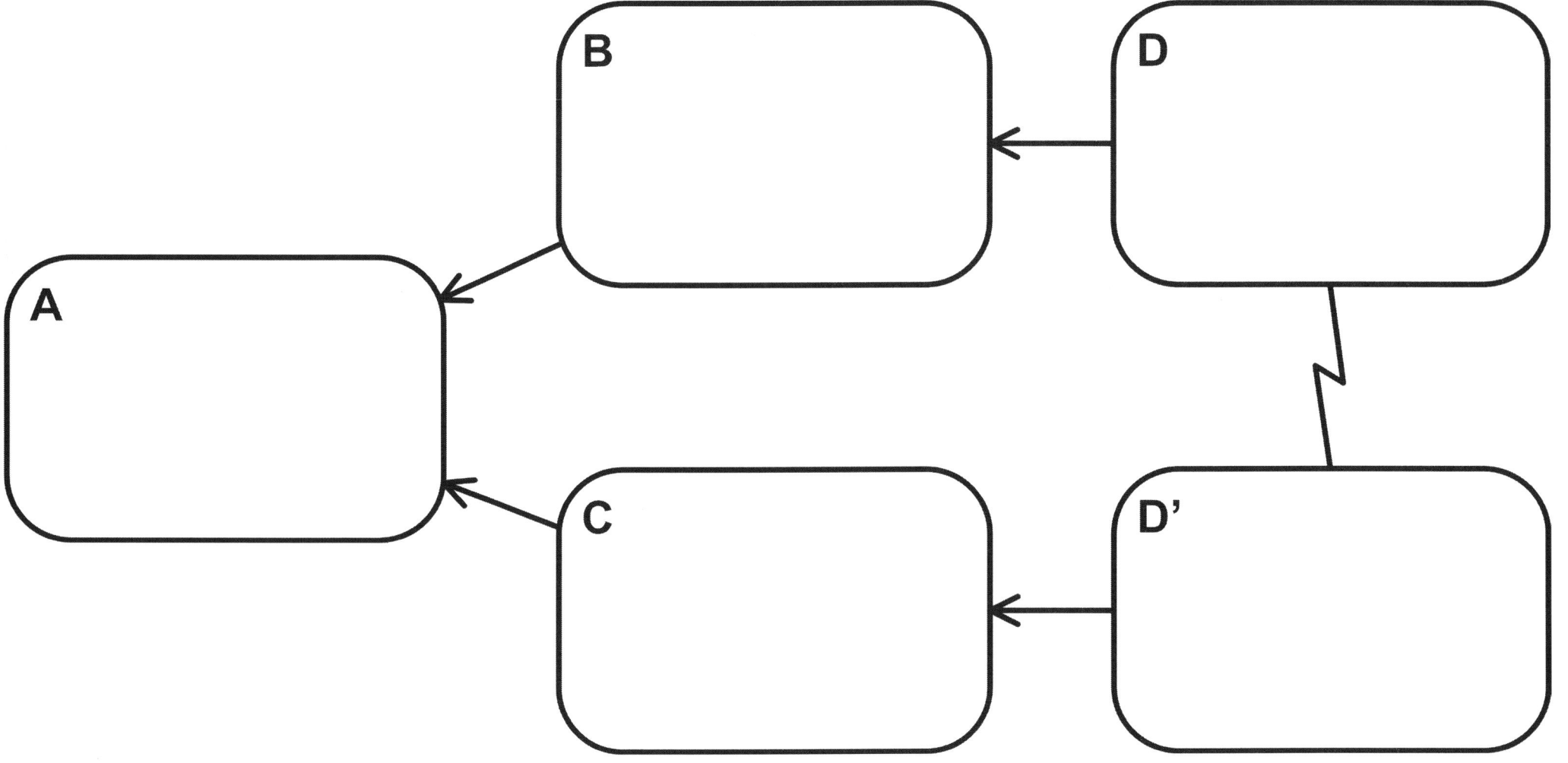

10.4.2 Fire Cloud — 2. outline

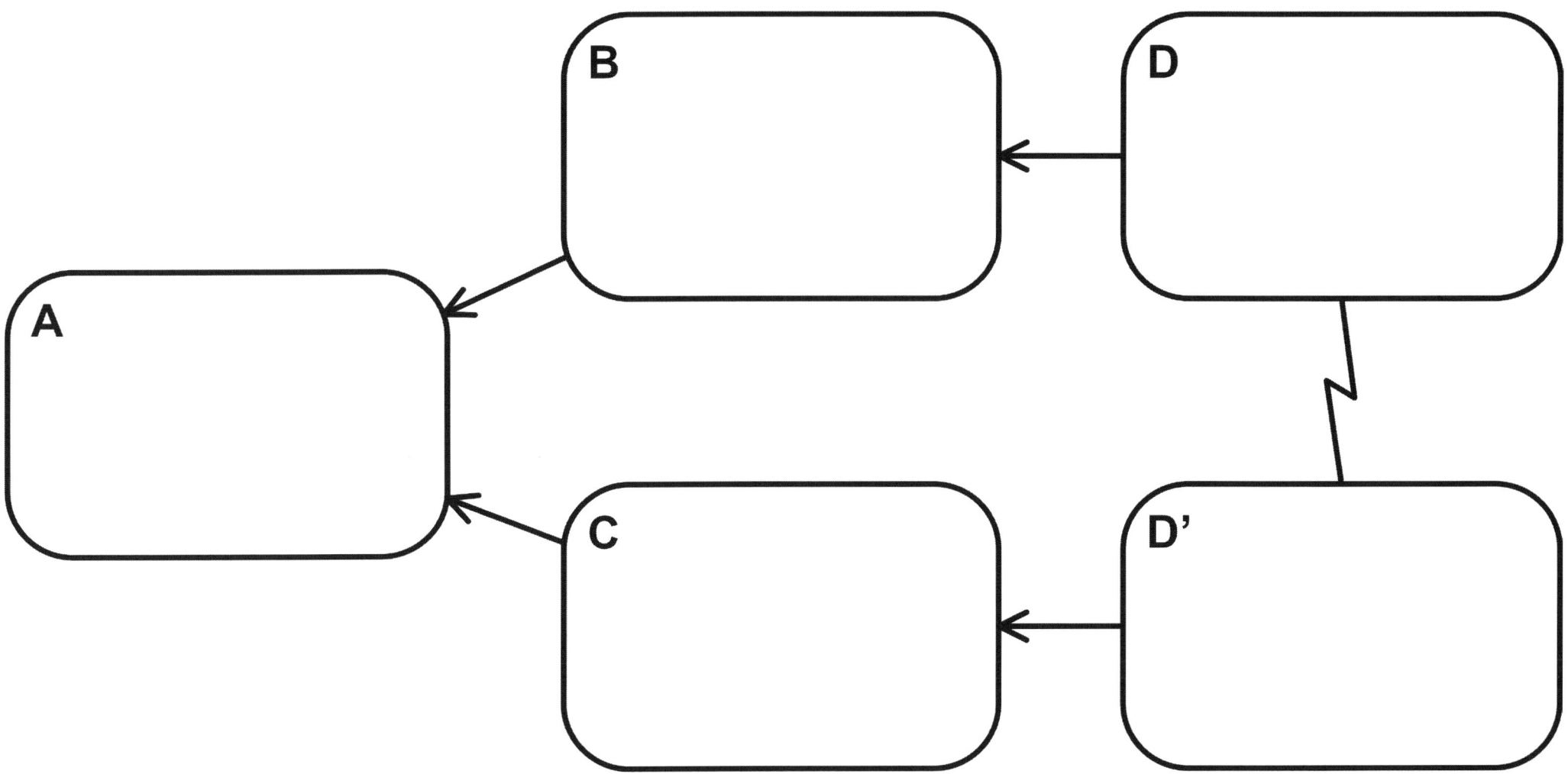

Workbook Win-Win Solutions

10.4.3 Fire Cloud with assumptions

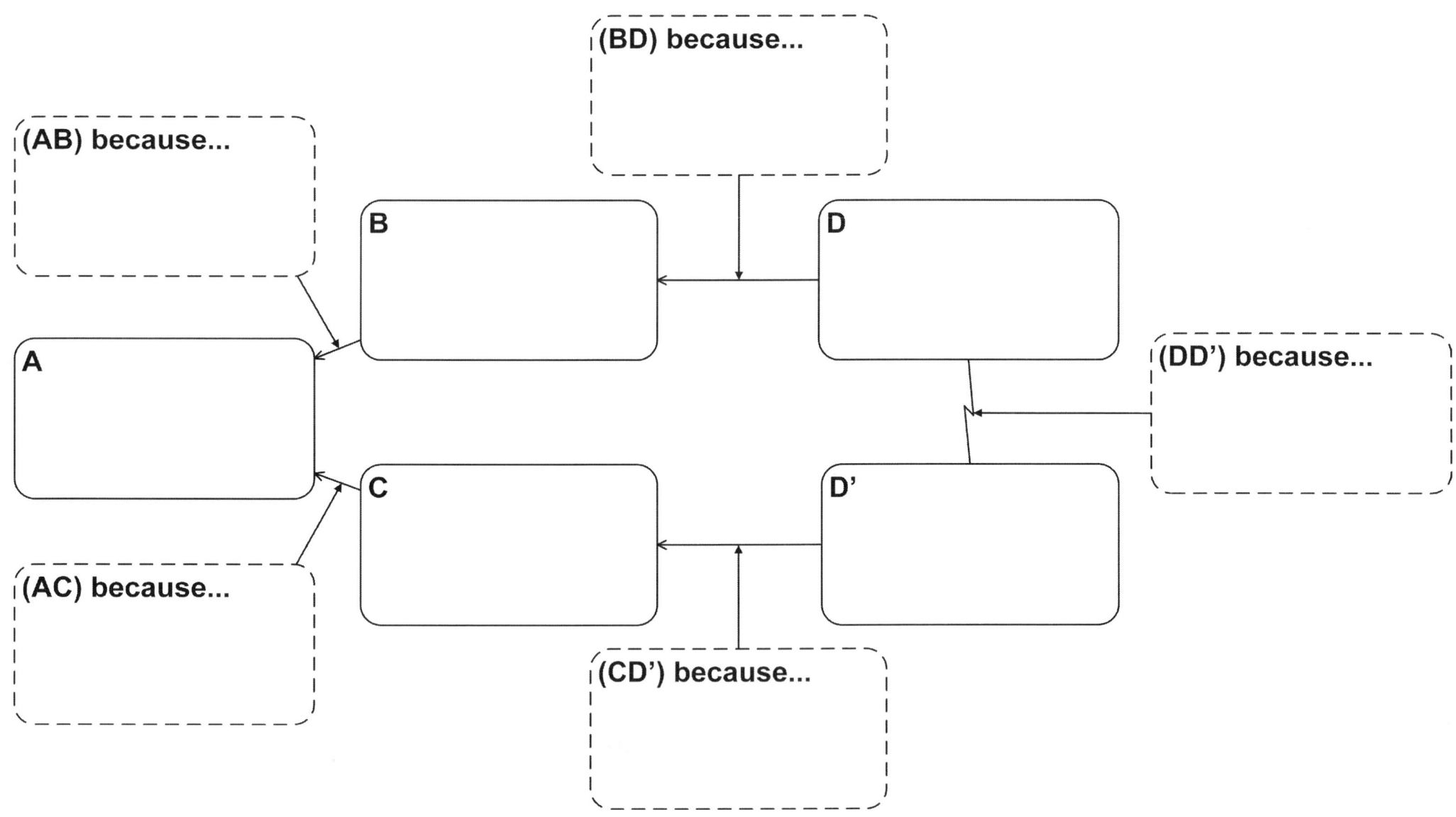

10.5 Possible solutions for B-D

Reasons / assumptions	Possible solutions

10.6 Win-Win Solution

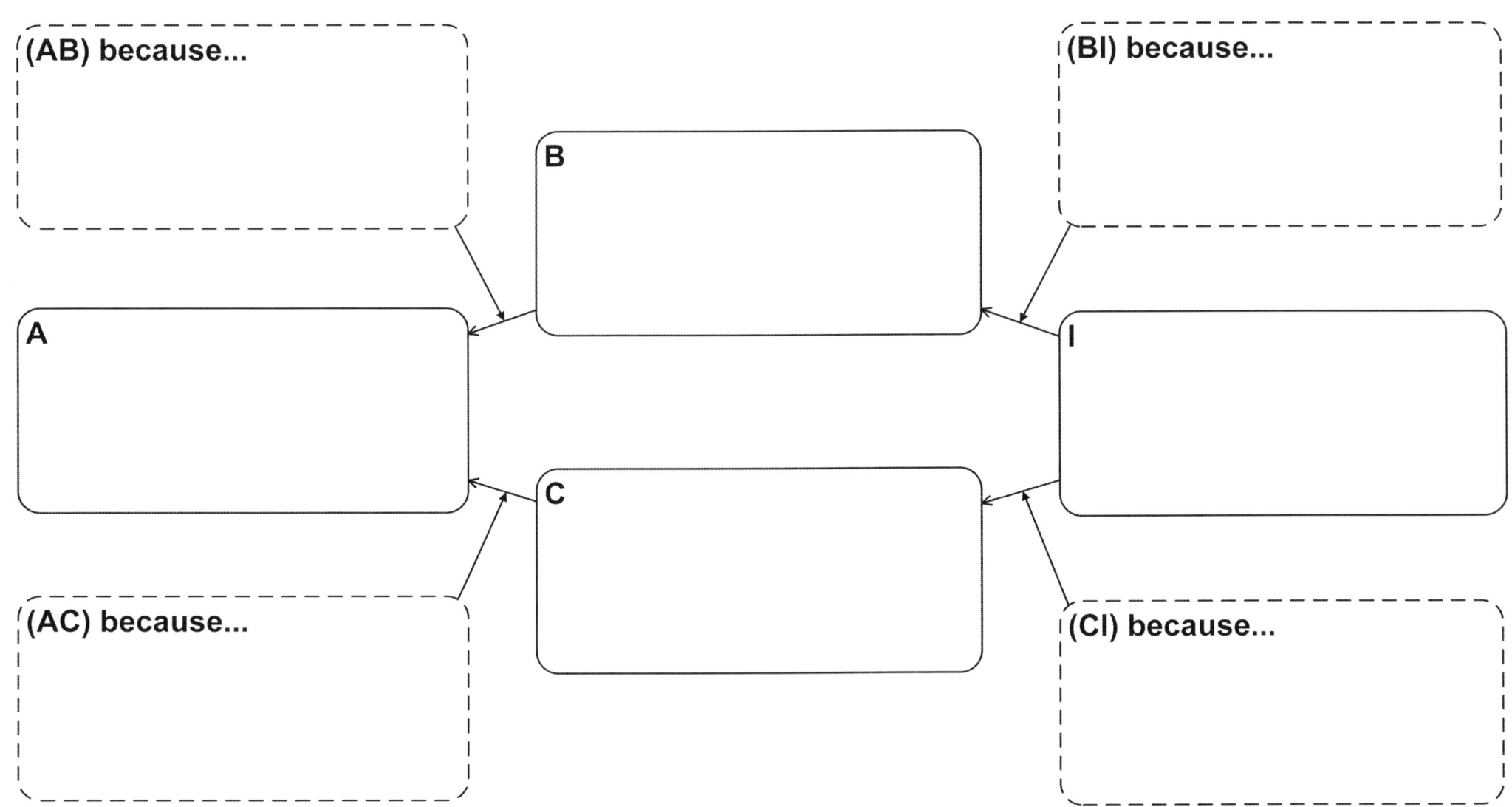

11 Fire—exercise 2

11.1 My fire report

Title / topic	
Report	

11.2 Fire Cloud

11.2.1 Fire Cloud—1. outline

Note: You will probably end up revising your formulations several times. Therefore, it might be a good idea to use sticky notes initially, instead of writing directly on the paper. Alternatively, you can revise your formulations on the following pages.

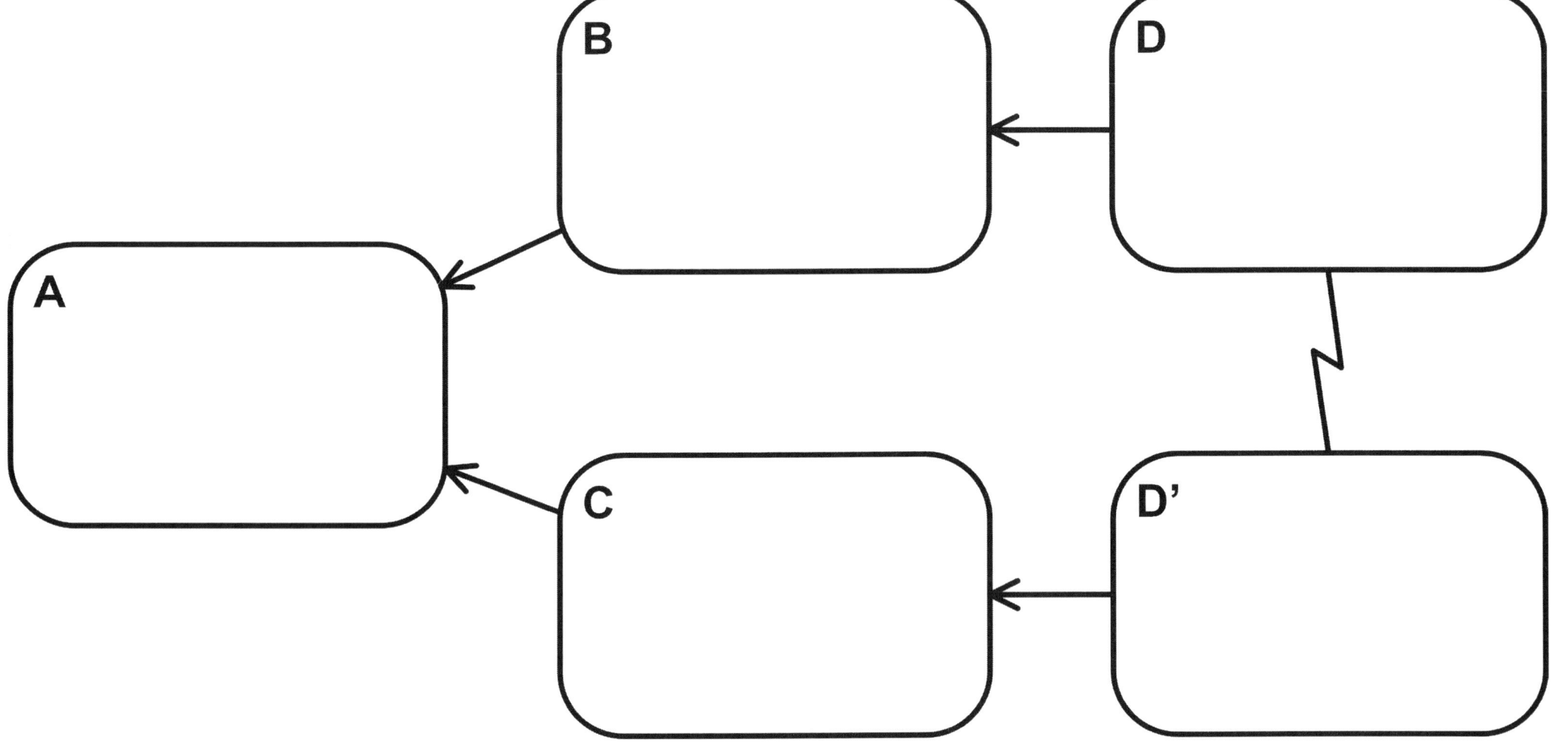

11.2.2 Fire Cloud — 2. outline

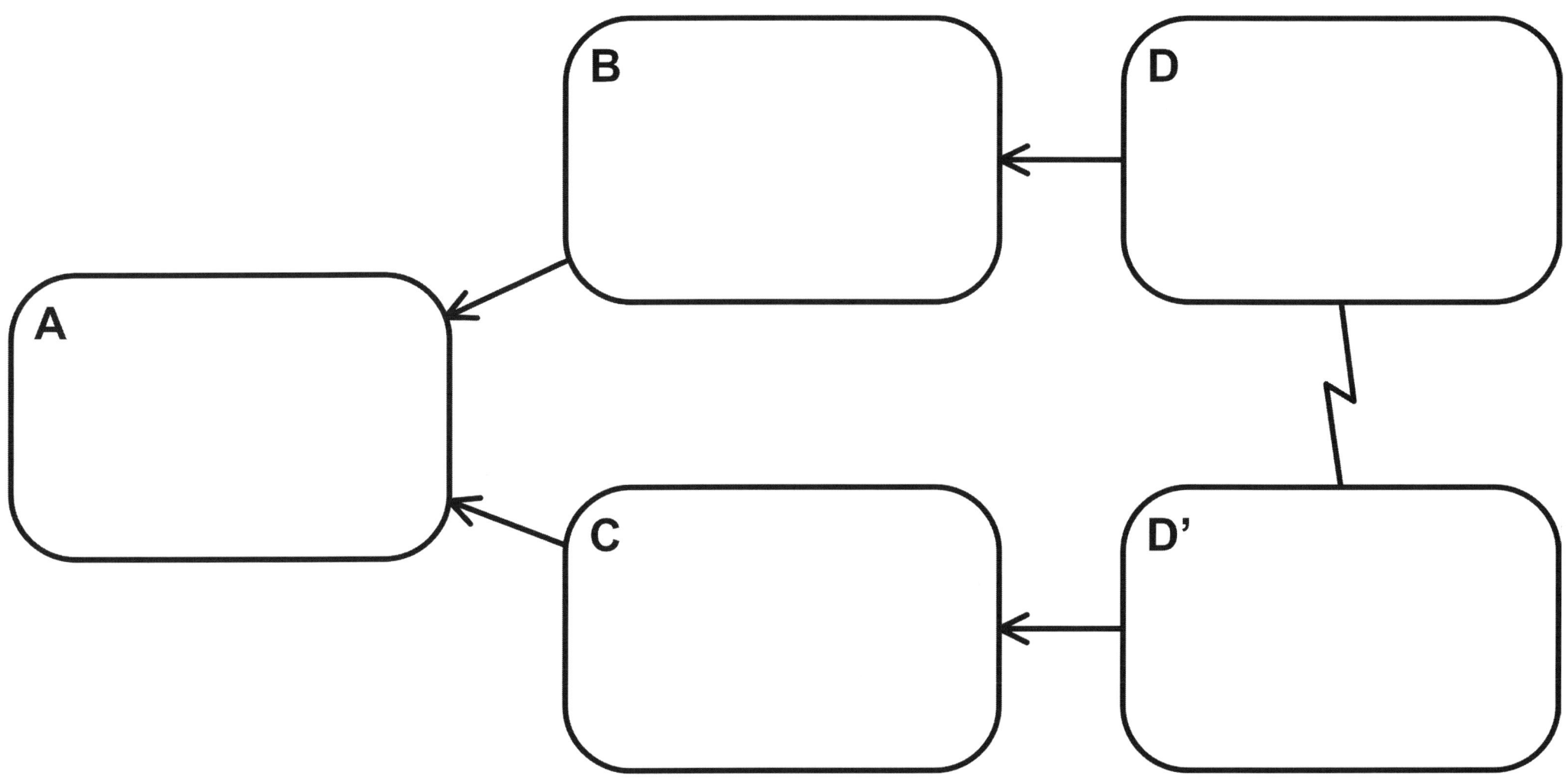

11.2.3 Fire Cloud with assumptions

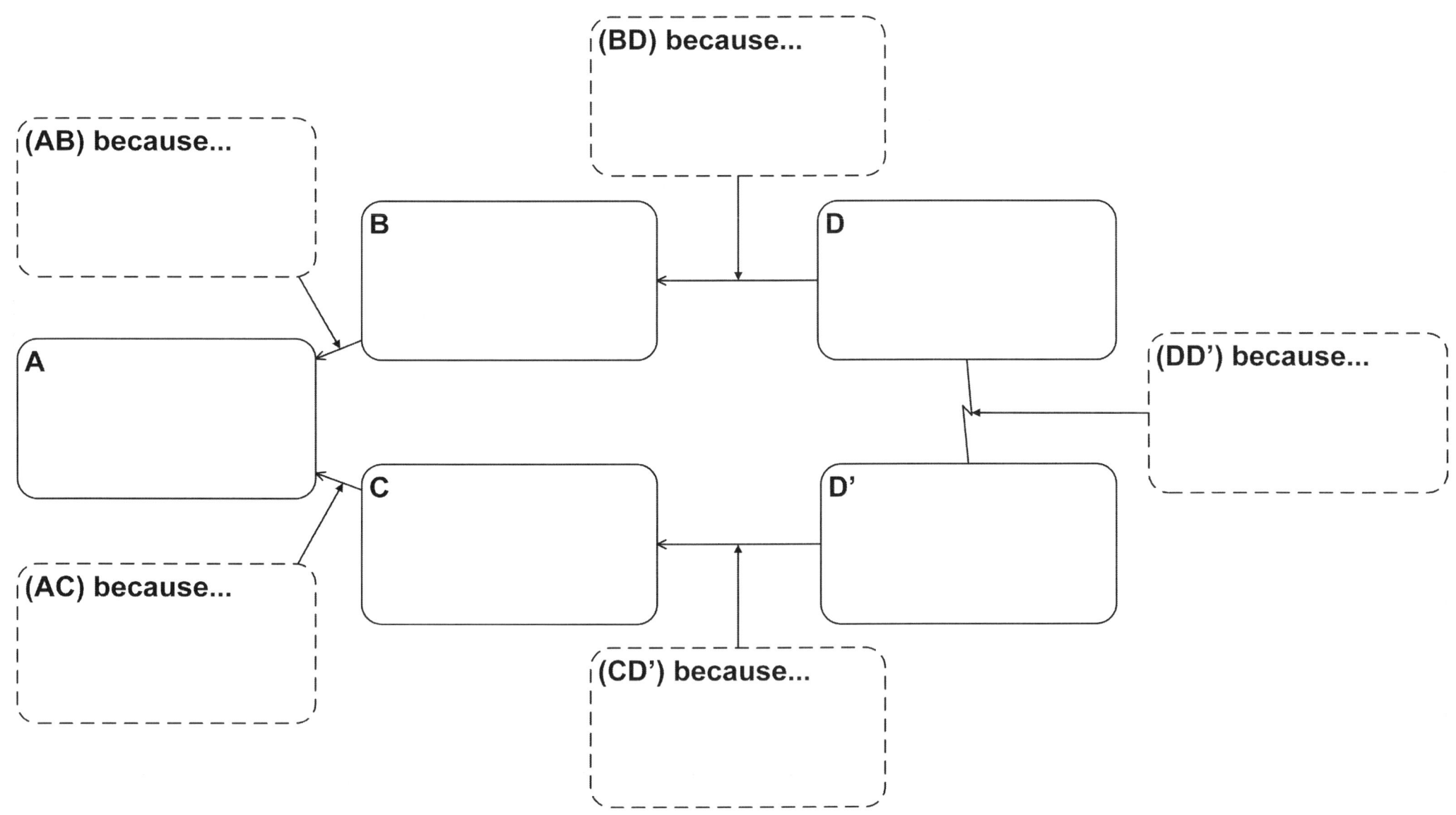

11.3 Possible solutions for B-D

Reasons / assumptions	Possible solutions

11.4 Win-Win Solution

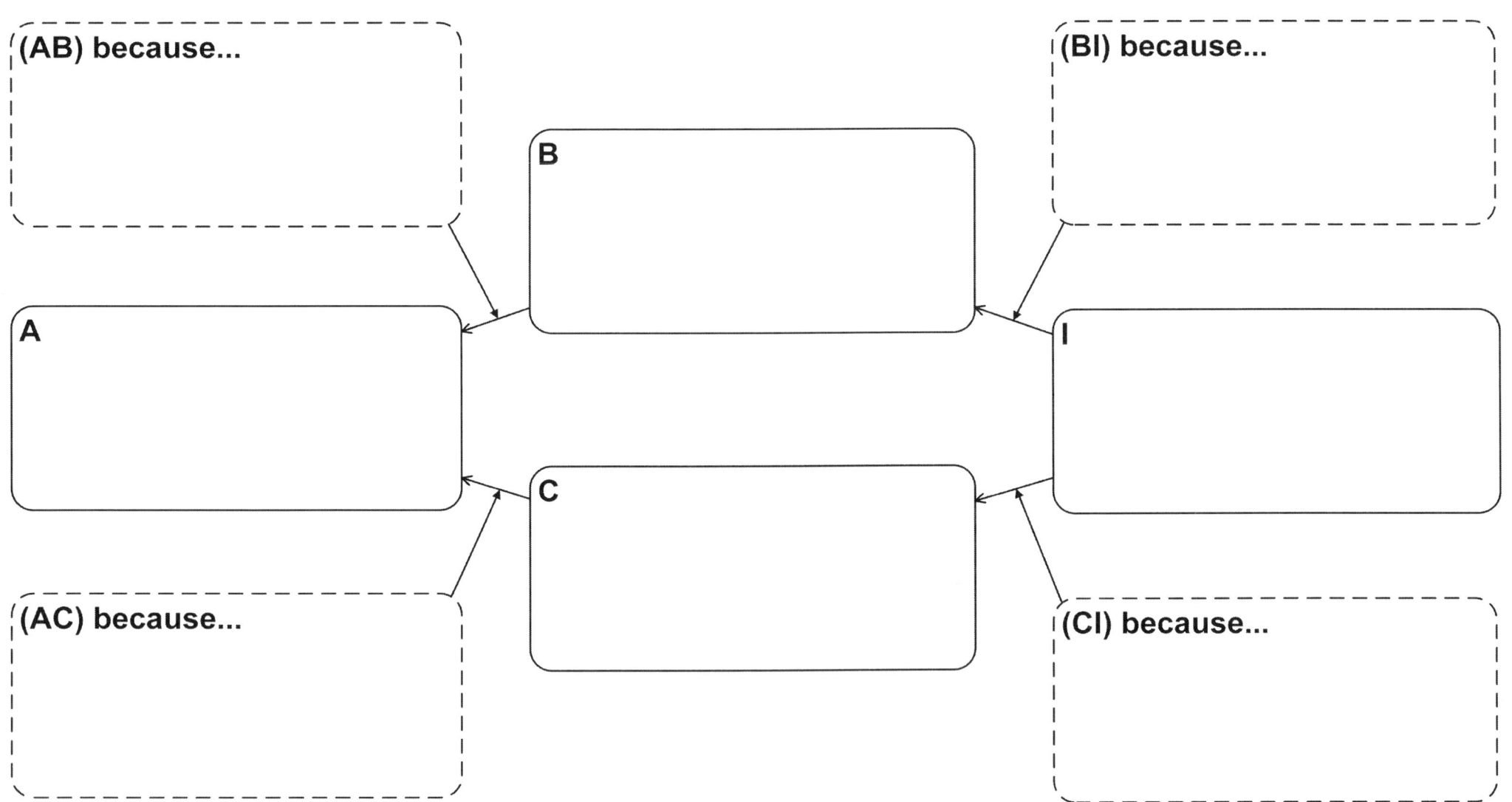

12 Fire — summary and completion

12.1 Human Resources Management

The key to successful leadership is rooted in appreciation.

The best way to find your own self-esteem is to appreciate others. However, appreciation does not come about by itself, giving appreciation is work in itself.

As in most companies and organizations, there will probably be many initiatives, rules, or projects in your environment that you do not fully agree with.

You can use 'Fire' to:

- detect and examine when your employees are incompatible with tasks, roles, or responsibilities, as well as competence or authority.
- detect and examine incompatibility of job, role or responsibility, as well as your own competence or authority.
- identify and change regulations that are no longer useful.

Use the Evaporating Cloud to solve conflicts with others on a factual level and to convey appreciation without losing face.

Make sure you don't start any fires, and practice fire prevention.

12.2 Method

1. Make the required decision immediately.

2. Then construct a Fire Cloud for yourself (alone) [sequence: C, D, D', B, A].

3. Introduce the Fire Cloud to the employee [sequence: A, C, D', D, B].

4. Together with the employee, identify the assumptions.

5. Together with the employee, resolve the connection between B and D.

6. Represent the win-win solution graphically.

12.3   Fire — overview

13 Conflict

13.1 What is a conflict?

A conflict between two people arises as a result of two conflicting needs: Two people face each other with mutually exclusive needs.

What would you do?

- Declare a state of war?
- Surrender?
- Enforce your solution?
- Evade the issue?
- Negotiate a compromise?

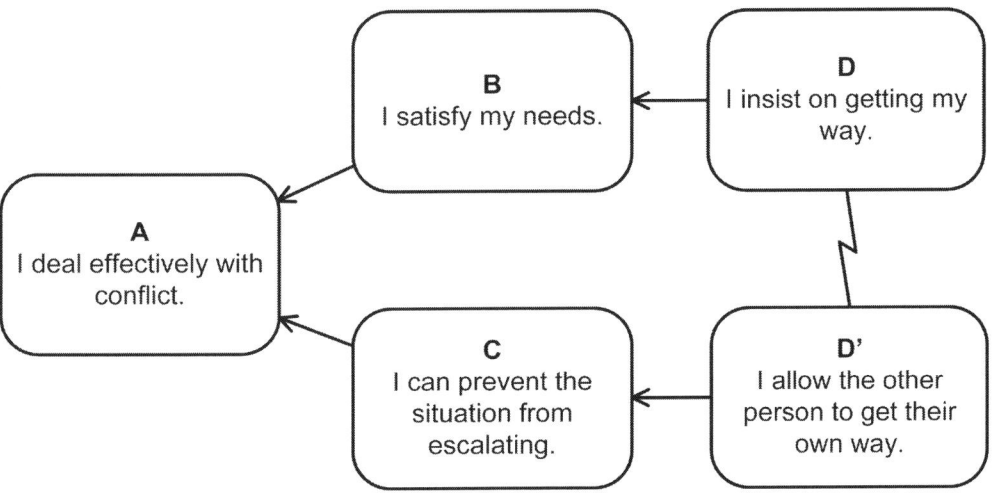

13.2 How can conflicts be resolved effectively?

We need to recognize the autonomy of both sides and assume that the respective target is legitimate. On the other hand, there is a unifying element, a common factor, which requires that both sides of the conflict cooperate with each other. If this were not the case, then there would be no conflict at all, because both sides could achieve their respective goals independently.

Taking this into consideration, the conflict can be solved by ensuring that the major objectives of both parties are achieved.

- Analyze the problem in a fair manner.
- Shift the focus from immediate 'wants' to the underlying goal.
- Find and define a common goal that has the objectives of both persons as necessary preconditions.
- Identify alternative solutions, which satisfy the important needs of both sides.

Change the 'what the other person wins, I've lost' attitude to 'there's a way we can both win'. So 'we are against each other' is no longer in the foreground, but is replaced instead with 'we are against the problem'.

What happens when you work on the Conflict Cloud now?

- You understand how you are involved in the conflict.
- You understand the other side of the conflict (empathy).
- You can check the emotional state of the action.
- You can avoid expressing feelings that might escalate the conflict.
- You can analyze the conflict fairly.
- You can focus on the core conflict that lies within the haze of the conflict.
- You will be able to build a bridge to communicate with the other side.

14 List of conflicts

14.1 Instructions

1. Create a list of five recent conflict situations.
2. Summarize each conflict in one sentence.

14.2 Recently encountered conflicts

	Conflict partner	Topic
1.		
2.		
3.		
4.		
5.		
6.		
7.		

For your first exercise, select a problem from this list, which is not chronic, is in the past and is completed.

15 Conflict—exercise 1 (with full instructions)

15.1 Report

15.1.1 Instructions

1. Write a report on your conflict—as if you were writing an essay or a letter of complaint. In the report, explain why this situation presents a problem, and how you and your services will be/were affected.

2. Take into account the following questions:
   - Who are the participants?
   - What happened?
   - When did it happen?
   - Where, and in what environment did the conflict occur?
   - What did I want to do? Why?
   - What should I not do? Why?

3. The purpose of the Conflict Report is to help you put the facts and your thoughts on the selected problem down on paper, so they can be subsequently processed and structured.

15.1.2 My conflict report

Title / topic	
Report	

15.2. Create a Conflict Cloud

Create a Conflict Cloud from the template on the following page.

15.2.1 Instructions

1. Transfer your conflict partner's desired action into field D and your desired action into box D'

2. In box C write down the need that you (will) satisfy by action D'.

3. Check the logic using the formula '(to achieve) C, I have to (do) D' '.

4. In box B write the need that your conflict partner probably satisfies (or will satisfy) by action D.

5. Check the logic using the formula '(to achieve) B, I have to/my partner has to/the company has to (do) D'.

6. In field A, write down the common goal: Why are B and C so important? What achievements do B and C have in common? What is the common/ultimate goal? What unites us?

7. Check the logic using the formula:
    - In order (to achieve) A, we need to (ensure) B.
    - In order (to achieve) B, we need to (do) D.
    - In order (to achieve) A, we need to (ensure) C.
    - In order (to achieve) C, we need to (do) D'.

8. Adjust the formulations, so they are 'coherent' and represent the conflict clearly.

9. Finally, carry out cross-matching. The action in D endangers need C, conversely, act D' endangers need B. Endangered in this respect means the likelihood of satisfying the need on the other branch significantly decreases, even if it is possible to achieve it under certain circumstances.

15.2.2 Our conflict — 1. outline

Note: You will probably end up revising your formulations several times. Therefore, it might be a good idea to use sticky notes, instead of writing directly on the paper. Alternatively, you can revise your formulations on the following pages.

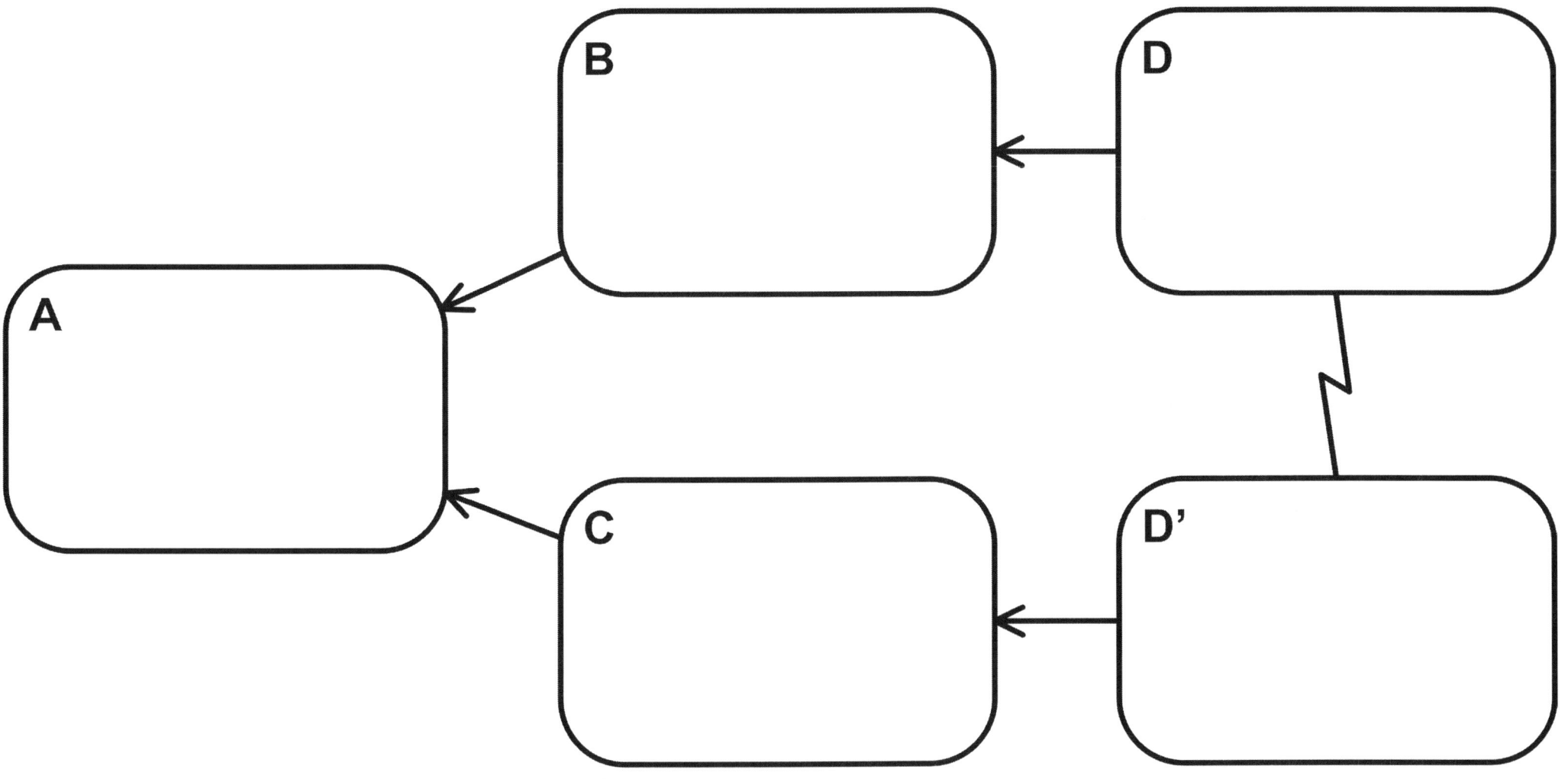

15.2.3 Our conflict — 2. outline

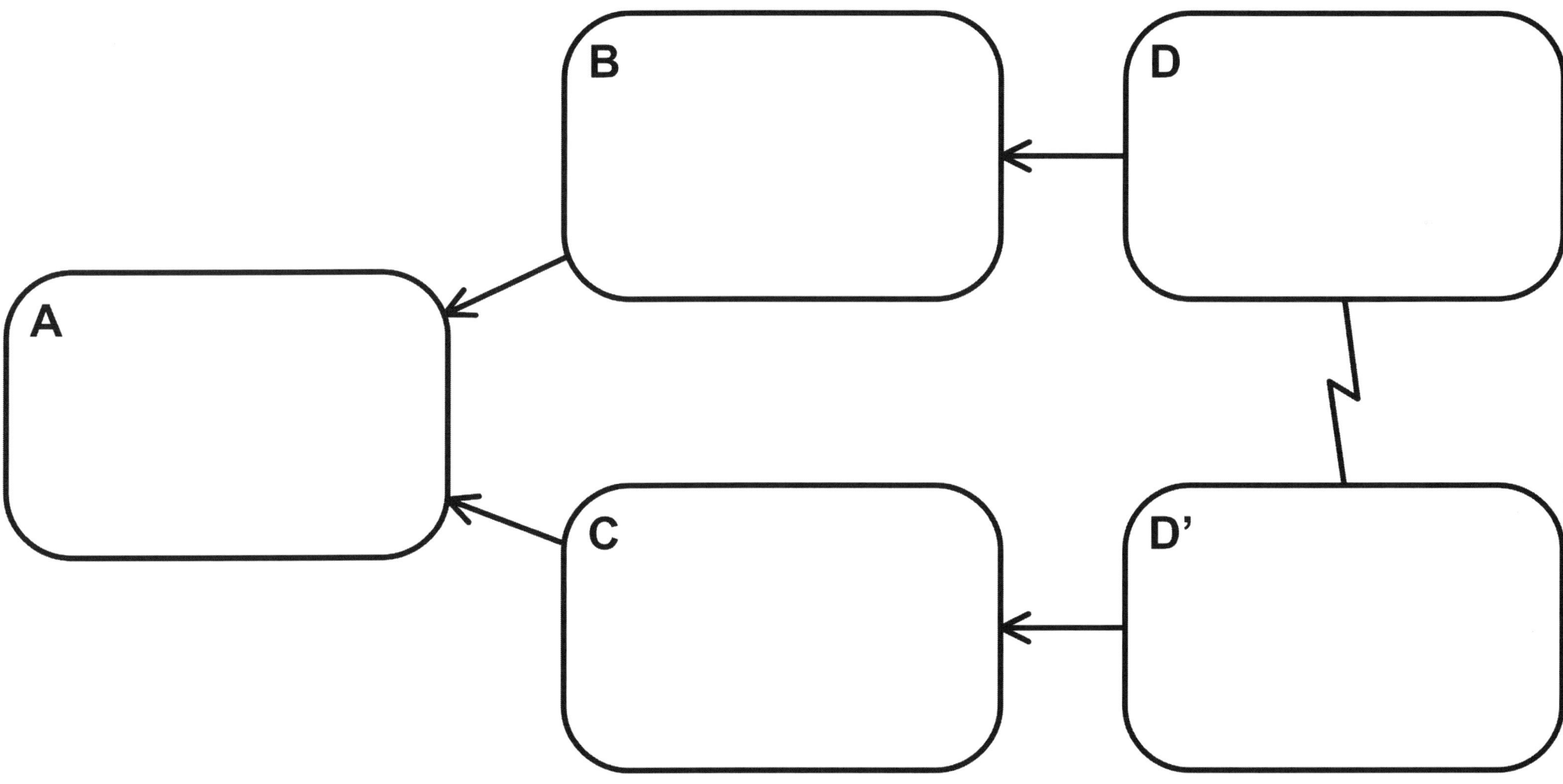

15.3 Assumptions

15.3.1 Instructions

There are good reasons for carrying out D in order to achieve B. There are also good reasons for carrying out D' in order to achieve C. These reasons are stored as assumptions in our thoughts, but often not spoken out loud. In order to consider them and understand them more accurately, we need to write them down. The assumptions need to explain the relationship between the elements and not just be reformulated in other words. The more assumptions you can find, the better; assumptions are a valuable source of possible solutions.

1. Make a note of the reasons why your conflict partner D has to carry out D in order to achieve B. To do this, complete this sentence: 'To achieve B, I need to do D, because...'. This formulates why B can only be achieved through action D. Find at least three, preferably five such reasons.

2. Repeat this step for the relationship between D' and C (your view of things), B and A, as well as between C and A.

3. Write down reasons why it is a dilemma at all, and why the problem is not solvable for you. Why are D and D' mutually exclusive? Find at least three, preferably five such reasons.

15.3.2 Conflict with assumptions

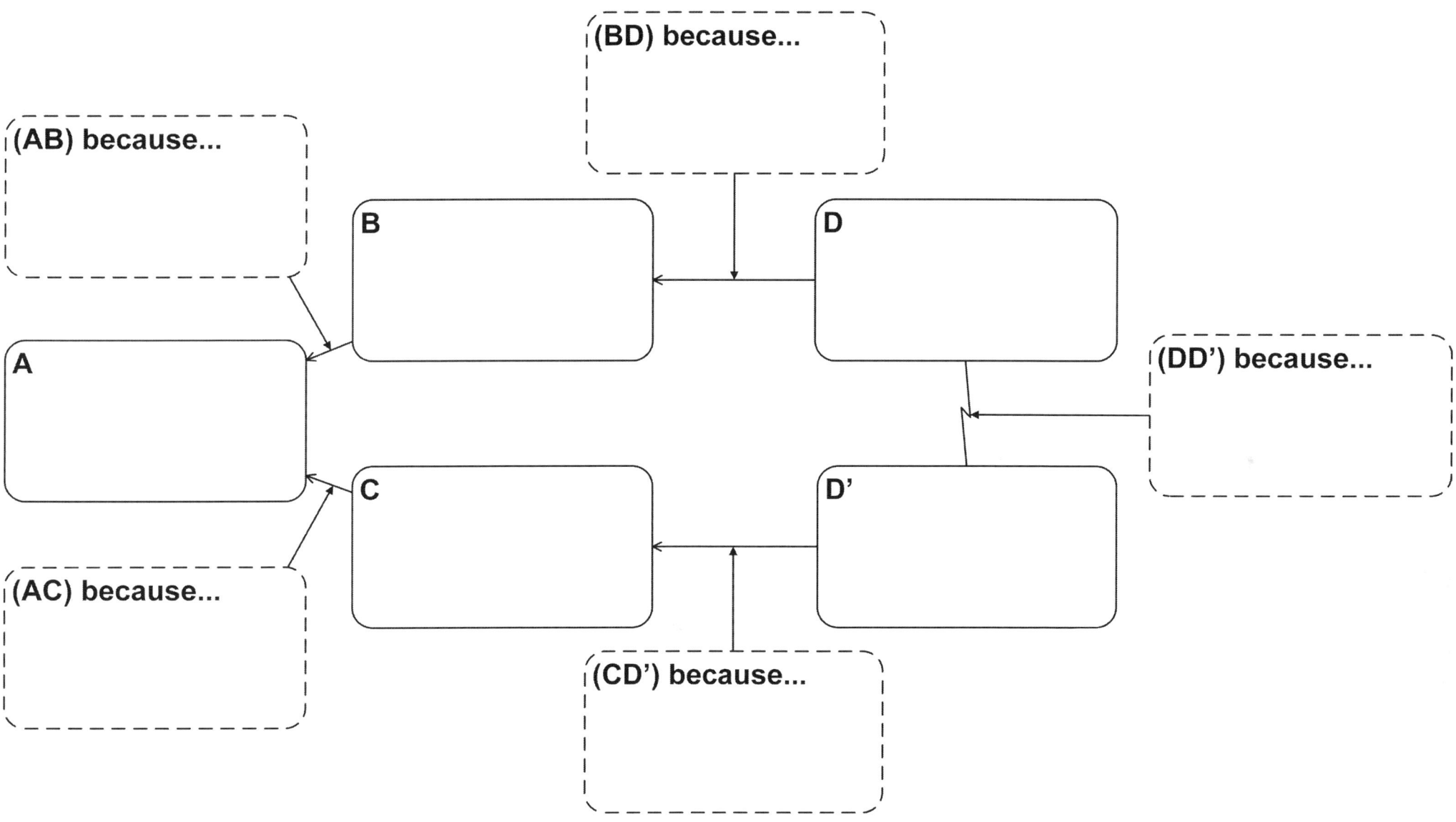

15.4 Possible approaches with conflict partners

15.4.1 I present the other person's Cloud

- First go through the other person's branch.
- Ask to see whether you have really understood it.
- Amend assumptions and reformulations.

15.4.2 I develop the Cloud with the other person

- First edit the other person's branch.
- Ask if there is anything you don't understand.
- Then edit 'your' page.

15.4.3 Independently

- Move the focus from 'wanted' to 'needed'.
- Let the other person suggest a solution.

15.5 Find possible solutions

15.5.1 Instructions

1. Transfer the two strongest grounds/arguments for A-C, A-B, B-D, C-D', D-D ' into the overview on the next page.

2. If there is a way to resolve or convert the reasons for the dilemma then the problem will resolve itself. To successfully do this, we need to find a new assumption and integrate it into the system. Therefore: Write down the possibilities that could follow, if the reasons/assumptions were negated/converted. Tips:

   - Search for erroneous (or very weak) assumptions.
   - Formulate assumptions as absolute statements
   - What assumptions contradict fundamental organizational goals?
   - Search for a reference environment in which the assumption is not required
   - Do not discard any idea/solution (injection), because it appears too difficult ('castles in the air' or 'pigs can fly'), or because you have already tried these
   - As a breakthrough, a solution can start with any of the prerequisite relationships (A-C, A-B, B-D, C-D ') and D-D'!
   - You should first examine B-D, C-D' and D-D'.

15.5.2 Our possible solutions

	Reasons / assumptions	Possible solutions
A-B		
A-C		
B-D		
C-D'		
D-D'		

Workbook Win-Win Solutions

15.6 Our solution

15.6.1 Our solution – 1. outline

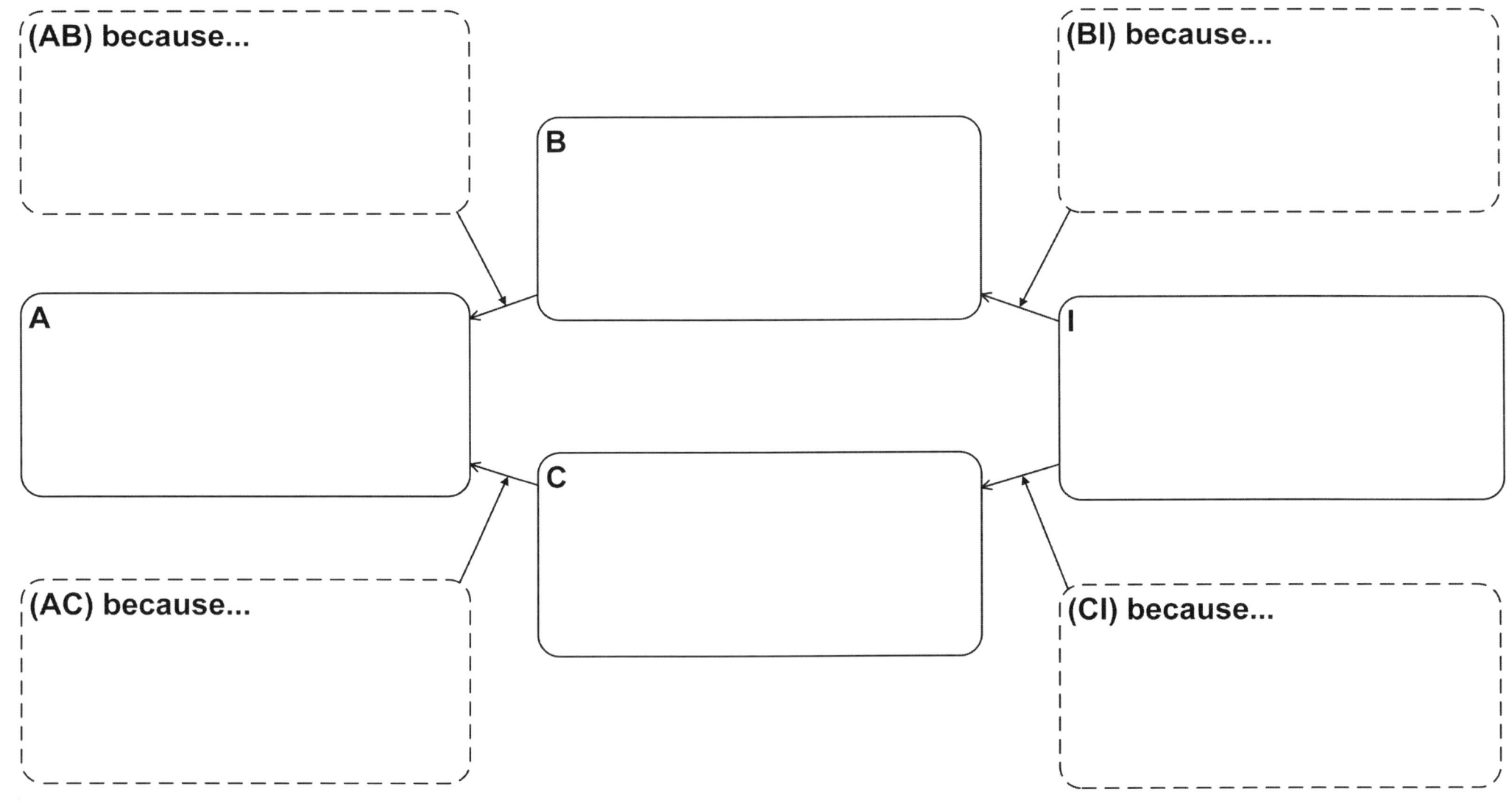

15.6.2 Our solution—2. outline

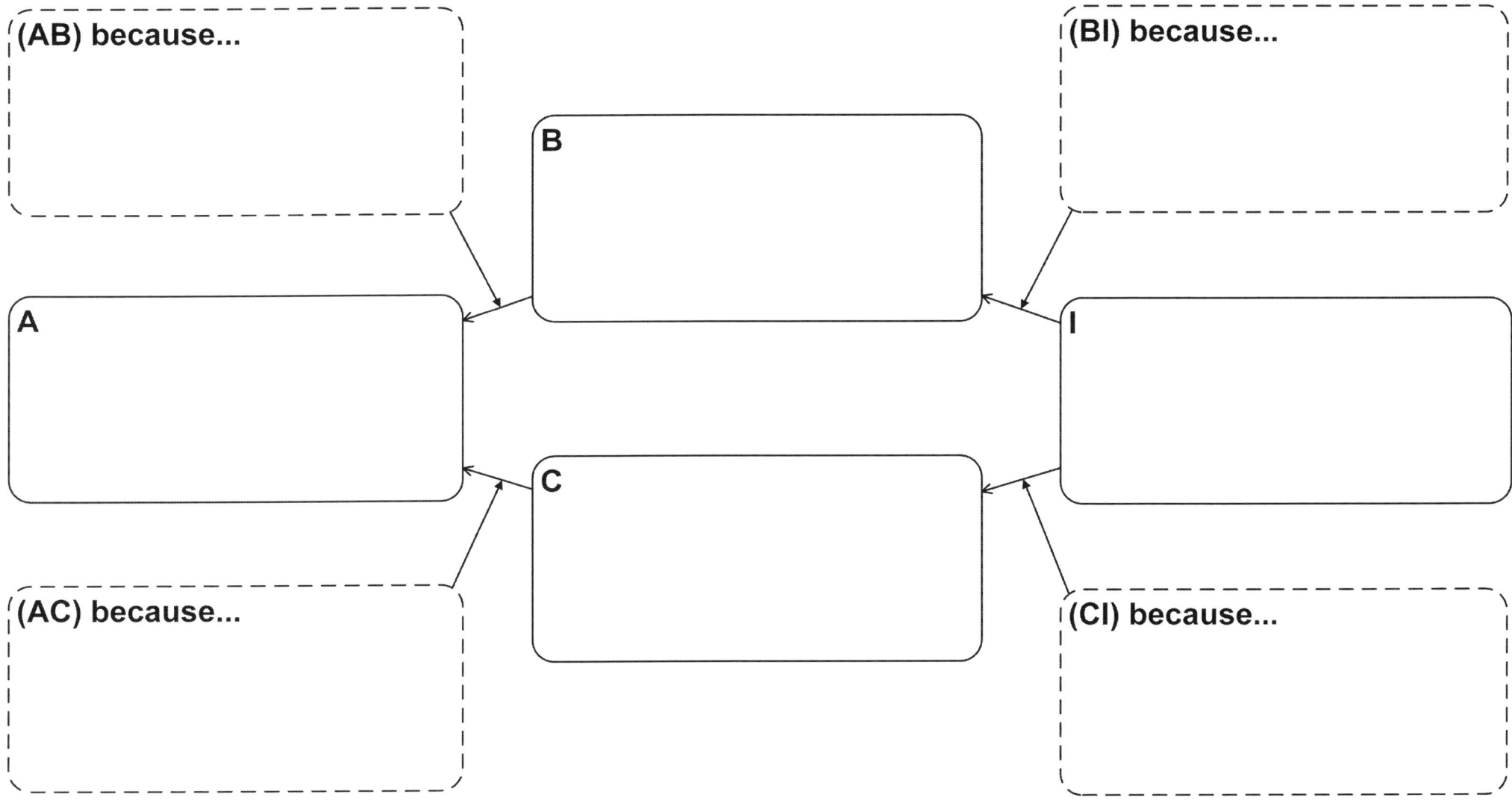

Conflicts 111

16 Conflict—exercise 2

16.1 Our conflict report

Title / topic	
Report	

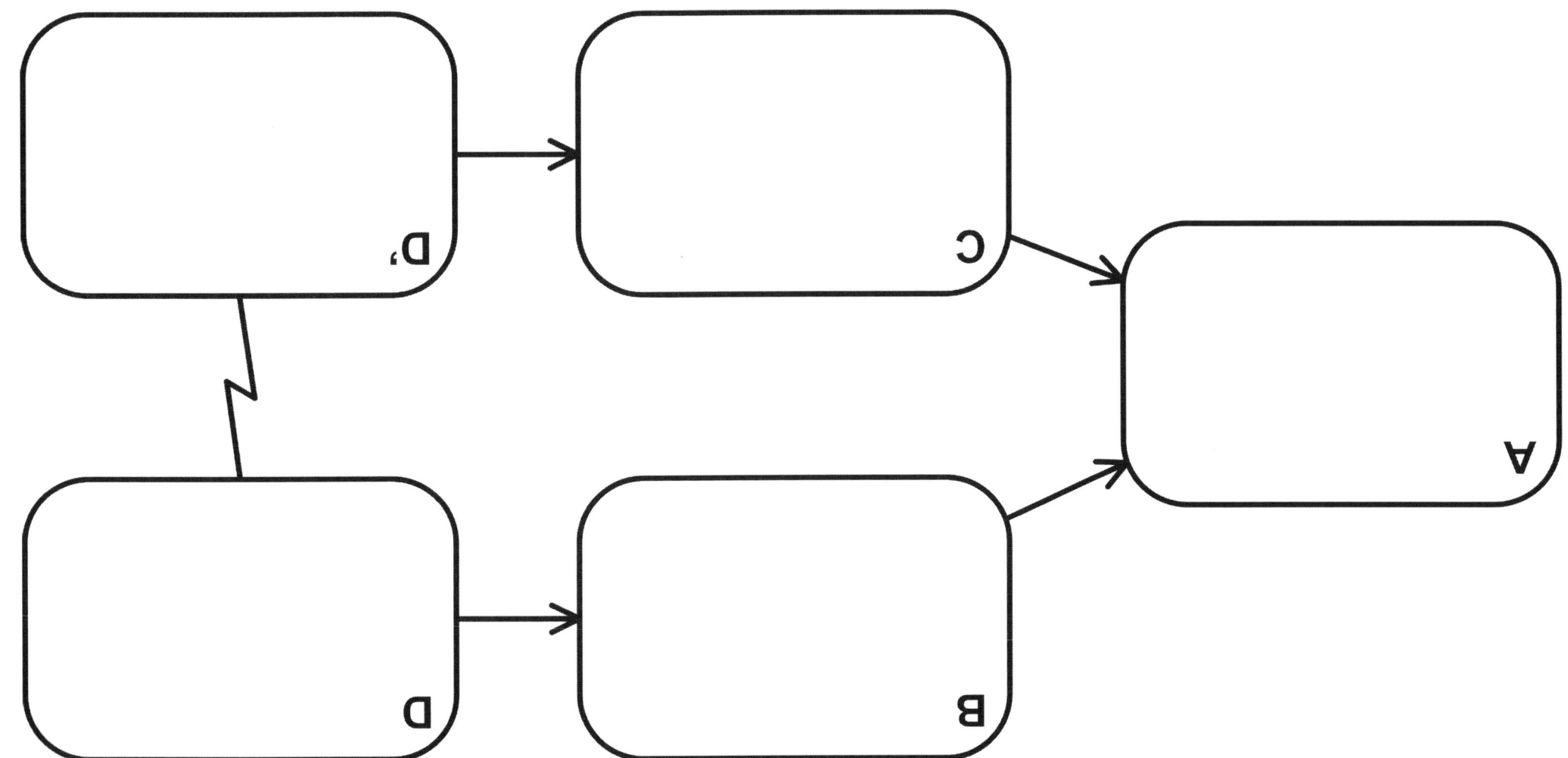

16.2 **Our Conflict Cloud**

16.2.1 Our conflict—1. outline

16.2.2 Our conflict — 2. outline

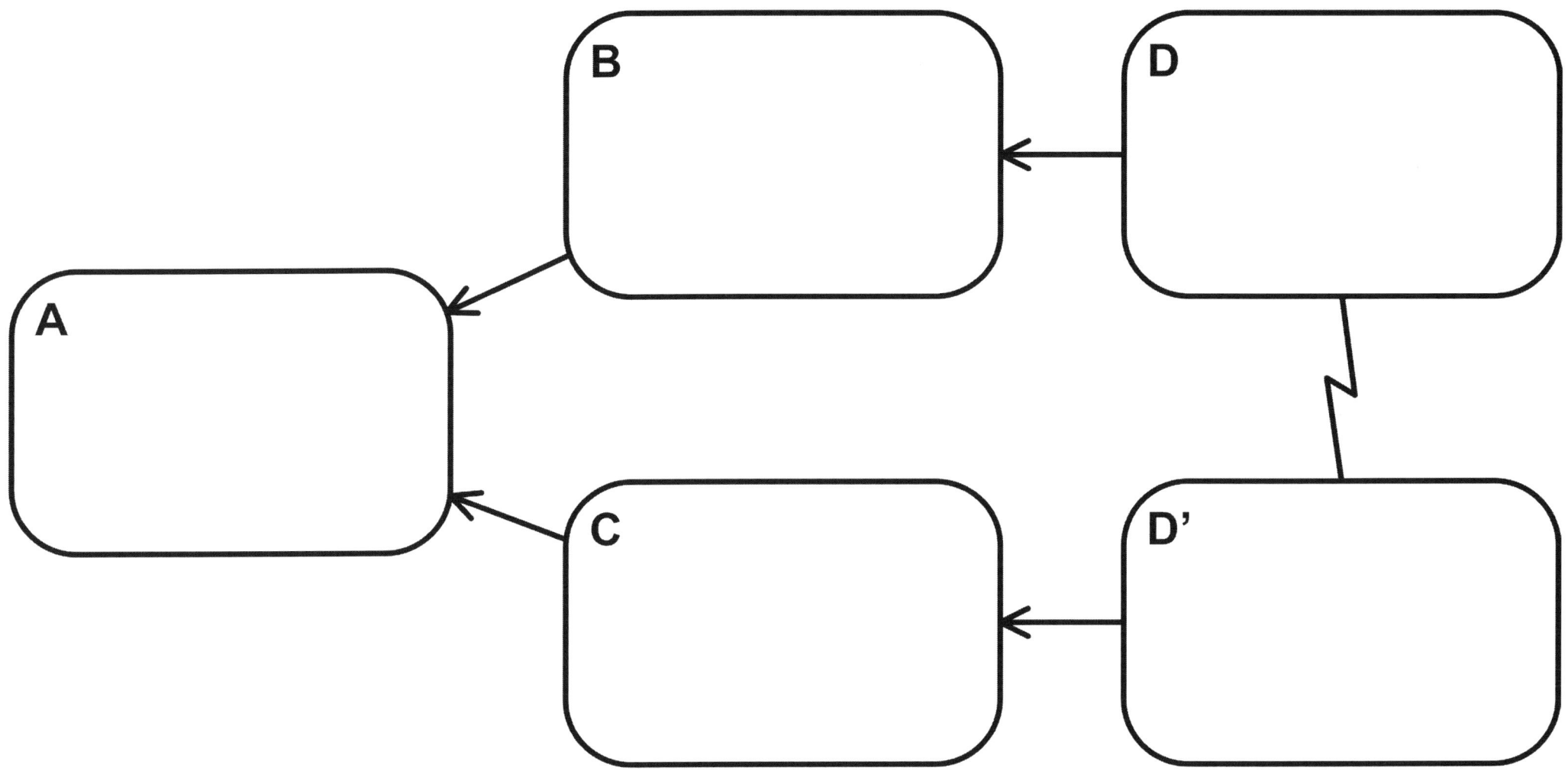

Conflicts

16.3 Conflict with assumptions

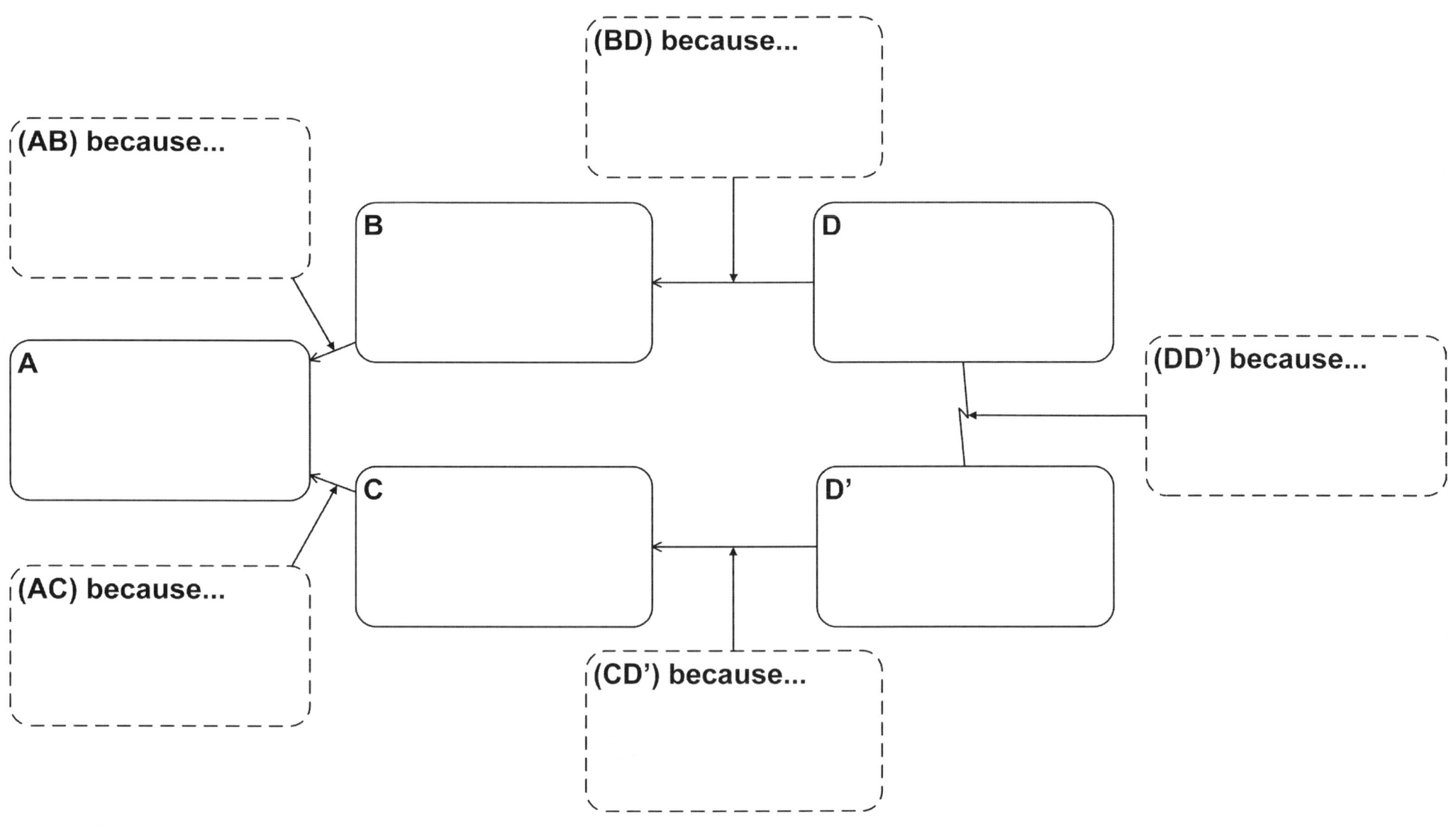

16.4 Our possible solutions

	Reasons / assumptions	Possible solutions
A-B		
A-C		
B-D		
C-D′		
D-D′		

Workbook Win-Win Solutions

16.5 Our solution

16.5.1 Our solution—1. outline

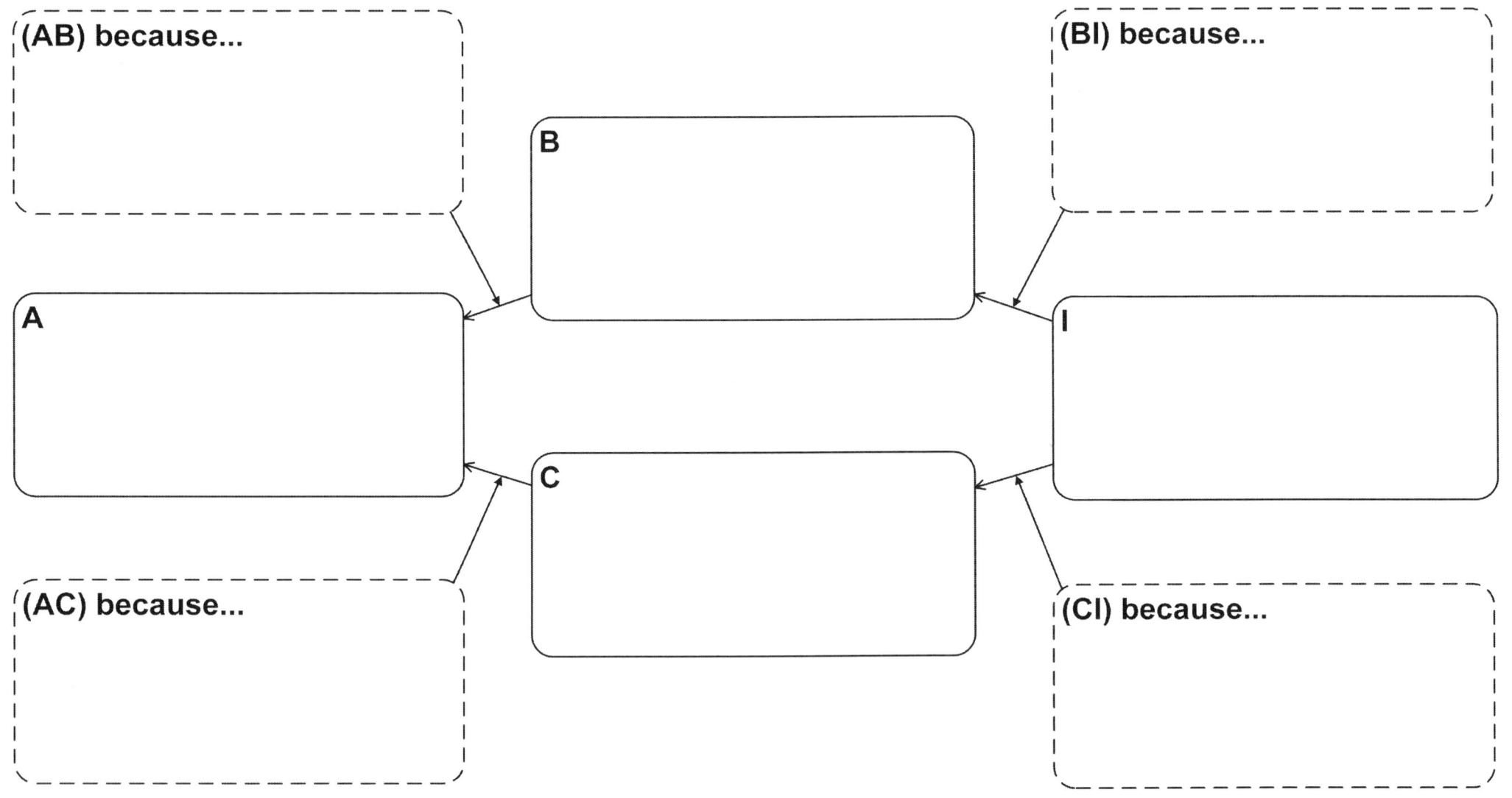

16.5.2 Our solution — 2. outline

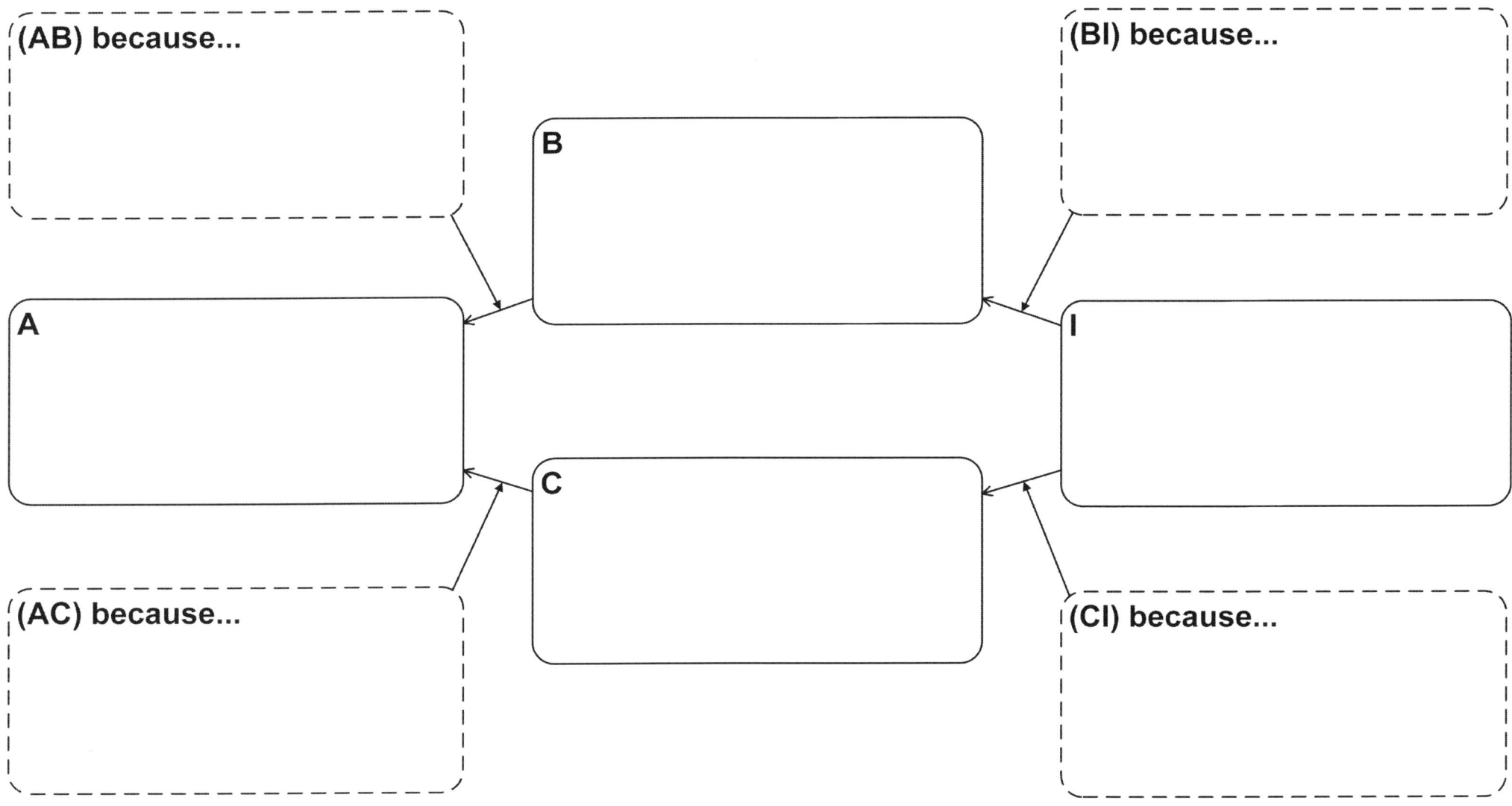

Conflicts

17 Presenting Clouds

17.1 Evaporating Cloud

Start with the target and present a full thread for each:

- To obtain (A), I need to ensure (C), because (A-C). To have (C), I must do (D'), because (C-D').
- To obtain (A), I need to ensure (B), because (A-B). To have (B), I must do (D), because (B-D).

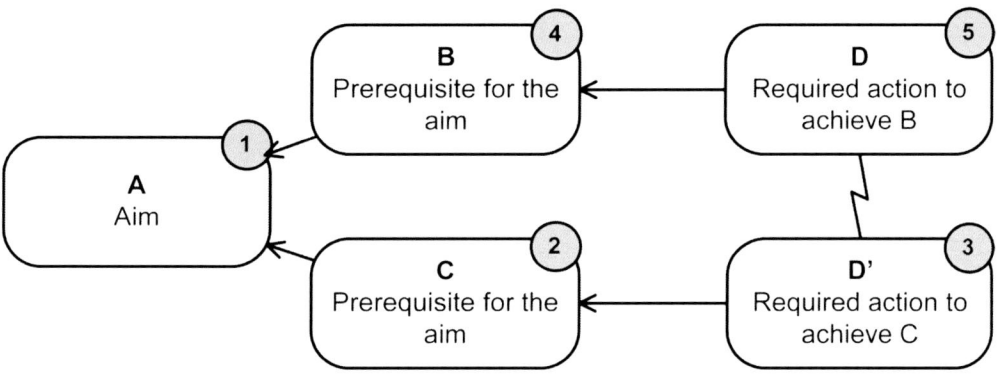

17.2 Fire Cloud

A provision or rule (D) prevents the person from doing something (D'), that they consider necessary to create the prerequisite (C) of aim (A). However, provision (D) was issued to ensure a different prerequisite (B) for aim (A). Start with the person's motive for the action.

- (C) is important. To achieve (C), you actually have to do (D'), because (C-D').
- But rule (D) prohibits doing (D'). D and D' are mutually exclusive, because (D-D').
- Rule (D) is used to ensure need (B) because (B-D).
- (B) and (C) are both required, to achieve aim (A), because (A-B) and because (A-C).

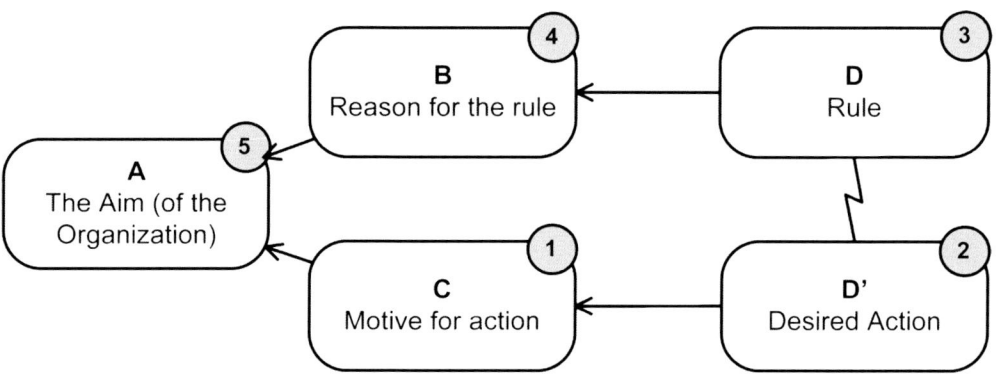

17.3 Conflict

First, present the other person's branch:

- (A) is an aim that is important to both of us.
- To obtain (A), you need to ensure (B) I assume your reasons for this are (A-B). To have (B), you have to do (D'), I assume your reasons are (A-B).
- To obtain (A), I need to ensure (C), because (A-C). To have (C), I must do (D'), because (C-D').
- (D) and (D') are mutually exclusive, because (D-D').

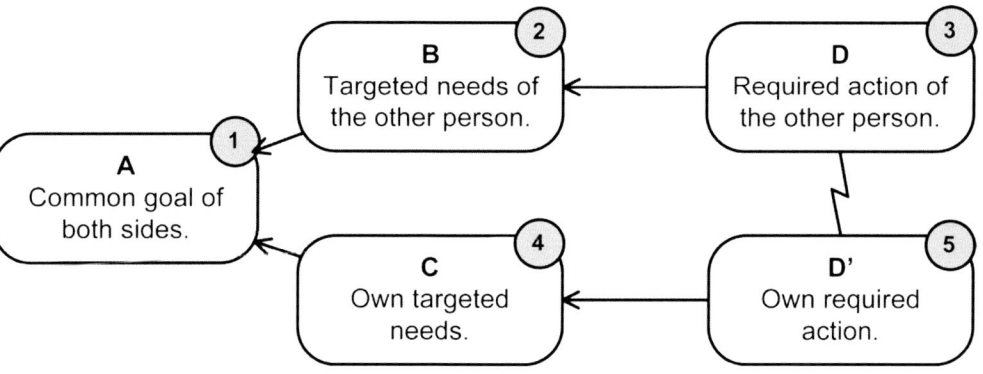

Conflicts 121

App recommendation

 The application **WinWinSolutions** aims to be a handy companion to solve your conflicts by using Conflict Clouds (or Evaporating Clouds) on your mobile phone or tablet. **Get it on Google Play.**

Book recommendation

Uwe Techt
Goldratt and the Theory of Constraints
The Quantum Leap in Management
190 pages, € 29.90

An introduction to the management system of the Theory of Constraints can be found in 'Goldratt and the Theory of Constraints. The Quantum Leap in Management' by Uwe Techt.
It contains an overview of the methods and applications of the Theory of Constraints in everyday language and is enriched with examples: Drum-Buffer-Rope, buffer management, critical chain project management, throughput accounting, pull distribution, irresistible offer, corporate strategy and viable vision. You will learn how to detect and use bottlenecks, how projects can reach their targets quickly and reliably, how competitive leads can be realized and turned into profit.

ISBN 978-3-8382-0697-4 [English-language edition]
ISBN 978-3-8382-0696-7 [German-language edition]
ISBN 978-3-8382-0901-2 [Spanish-language edition]

Uwe Techt
Projects that Flow
More Projects in Less Time
464 pages, € 39.95

Projects can go over budget, exceed deadlines, or deliver restricted features and quality. This can result in economic damage for companies and their clients.
The difficulties arise at source. Established metrics and management methods slow projects down by creating conflicts in operations and decision-making.

A radically new approach is needed; one that features
- simple, constraint-oriented management,
- clear, robust priorities,
- company-wide rather than locally focused optimization,
- a focus on speed, on ProjectsFlow.

ISBN 978-3-8382-0699-4 [English-language edition]
ISBN 978-3-8382-0651-6 [German-language edition]
ISBN 978-3-8382-0930-2 [Spanish-language edition]

VISTEM GmbH & Co. KG

Von-Siemens-Straße 1
64646 Heppenheim
Deutschland

Phone: +49 (6252) 79 53 07-0
Fax: +49 (6252) 69 90 79-9

www.vistem.eu
info@vistem.eu

**If you have questions or if you would like
to receive further information please get in touch.**